WHAT READERS AND CRITICS SAY ABOUT
❧ THE POETRY OF FELIX DENNIS ❧

'Felix Dennis writes wonderful poetry.'
— Janet Street-Porter, *journalist and broadcaster*

'Felix Dennis is the real thing. I love reading his verse and you will, too.'
— Stephen Fry, *actor, writer and director*

'The uncrowned Poet Laureate... he writes in the language of the soul.'
— Christopher Rush, *author*

'His poetry sings like a summer breeze through the fairground.'
— Sir Paul McCartney, *musician and songwriter*

'He is the very essence of English poetry — lyrical, rhythmic, emotional.'
— Jon Snow, *television newscaster*

'I love his poetry. With moments of real genius, some of his poems
will last as long as poetry is read.'
— Benjamin Zephaniah, *poet*

'If Waugh were alive, he would fall on Dennis's verse with a
glad cry of recognition and approval.'
— John Walsh, *The Independent*

'I enjoy his poetry immensely.'
— Mick Jagger, *singer and songwriter*

'The best poet writing in the English language.'
— Tom Wolfe, *critic and author*

WHAT READERS AND CRITICS SAY ABOUT
❧ THE POETRY OF FELIX DENNIS ❧

'An engaging monster, filled with contradictions and reeking of sulphur.'
— *The Times*

'He invokes sorrow as fast as regret, pain as readily as passion,
love as tenderly as murderous rage.'
— Shirley Conran OBE, *author*

'Beautifully crafted, accessible and unforgettable.
To watch him perform is pure magic.'
— Clare Fitzsimmons, *Stratford Observer*

'At least one of these poems will be instantly anthologised.'
— Melvyn Bragg, *broadcaster and author*

'Total, utter joy... so real, so readable and so enjoyable.'
— Richard Fair, *bbc.co.uk*

'Talent at once wise and maddeningly childish, optimistic and grim.'
— Dawn French, *actor and comedienne*

'You feel he lived it so richly, so dangerously to be so wise for our delight.'
— Dr. Robert Woof, *Director of The Wordsworth Trust*

'He makes it look easy, damn him! I couldn't put the book down.'
— Z. Menthos, *critic.org*

'Eloquently observant, beautifully crafted poetry.'
— Hannah Gal, *The Huffington Post*

I
JUST
STEPPED
OUT

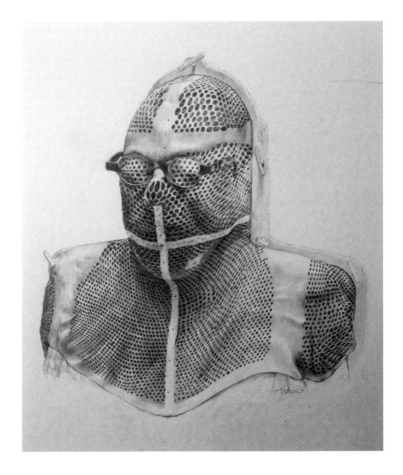

Felix Dennis strapped into his radiotherapy mask, 2012.
Illustration by Yanko Tihov

I JUST STEPPED OUT

Felix Dennis

EBURY
PRESS

13 5 7 9 10 8 6 4 2

Published in 2014 by Ebury Press, an imprint of Ebury Publishing

A Random House Group Company

The Random House Group Limited Reg. No. 954009

Addresses for companies within the Random House Group can be found at
www.randomhouse.co.uk

A CIP catalogue record for this book is available from the British Library

The Random House Group Limited supports The Forest Stewardship Council® (FSC®),
the leading international forest certification organisation. Our books carrying the
FSC label are printed on FSC® certified paper. FSC is the only forest certification scheme endorsed by
the leading environmental organisations, including Greenpeace.
Our paper procurement policy can be found at www.randomhouse.co.uk/environment

Cover Photography: Simon Turtle
Hardcover and Endpapers Illustration: Nick Hardcastle
Designer: Rebecca Jezzard
Production: Caroline Rush

Printed by The Westdale Press Limited

Set in Hoefler Text

ISBN 9781785030031

To buy books by your favourite authors and register for offers, visit:
www.randomhouse.co.uk

To
my friends; past, present, and
perhaps even those in an
unknowable future.

to
the Daemon on my
shoulder for so many years
and
the Muse who came late but
made up for it.

Some go vicious,
Some go wise,
The saddest like a robot,
The best with starlight in their eyes —
Though where they go,
I know not.

— *'Knowing When To Go'*

Not all things go wrong —
and after
Winter's famine comes the spring;
Kindness, beauty,
children's laughter —
Joy is ever
on the wing.

— *'Not All Things Go Wrong'*

I JUST STEPPED OUT

Where am I? — Oh, I just stepped out,
No need to make a fuss, or shout,
No need to comb the nearest wood
Or roam about the neighbourhood.

Call off the dog — she'll find no scent,
Please don't worry where I went,
And do not climb the garden tree,
My dear, you'll catch no glimpse of me.

The attic steps will pinch your thumb,
The cellar will be dark and dumb,
Yet should you search your heart with care,
Though I am gone, you'll find me there.

Soho, London June 15, 2007

'Beware the words of dying men. They are lies, embellishments,
requests for favours or prophetic — none fit for the ears of mortals.'
    — from the author's unfinished play, 'The Wise Fool'

'Marion, as you can see, I am dying.' 'Yes, I'm afraid you are, my dear.'
'So is there any chance of a quick blowjob?'
    — cartoonist Edward Barker to his friend Marion Hills
        from his hospital deathbed, April 1997

This is a peculiar collection of verse. Perhaps unique in one sense — as a Verse Diary begun on the day before I learned that I had contracted cancer in both lungs and had only a short while to live.

The diagnosis of my lung cancer is a peculiar tale, told in the note attached to the poem 'Queer Interlude' — a diagnosis made weeks, even months in advance of the normal pattern of events when symptoms in a patient (as doctors put it) first 'exhibit' themselves. This meant that I was blessed — or cursed — with a prolonged foreknowledge that most terminally ill patients are denied.

I decided to use the time available to attempt to write a poem every day, or every two or three days, at least while I was capable of doing so; poems to chart my physical, emotional and psychological journey. That the first poem in my Verse Diary, 'Too Much Is Going Right', was completed on the day before I received my diagnosis (and then sat down, a gibbering wreck, to pen 'A Shadow On My Lung') is scarily prophetic. Or is it? Statisticians or those of a narrow scientific bent will likely pooh-pooh this as coincidence. I am not so sure the rest of us could, would, or even should do so.

Born in a nursing home in Kingston upon Thames, Middlesex, just after midnight on 27th May, 1947, I shall die, in all probability, at my 16th-century thatched house, The Old Manor, Dorsington, a small hamlet near Stratford-upon-Avon, Warwickshire — probably at some point in 2014.

My ambitious, working-class mother, Dorothy, (now in her mid-nineties and whom I suspect I shall sadly predecease) was training to be a bookkeeper when she gave birth to me, her first son. She later became an accountant, an unusual achievement for someone born and raised in a terraced home without electricity or a bathroom. Some of her brothers and sisters mocked her because she insisted on speaking the 'received' English she had heard listening to the BBC. My father, Reginald Dennis, was an RAF navigator who spent much of World War II ferrying supplies by air over high mountain ranges from Dum-Dum in India to General Slim's army in Burma.

Following the war, Reg and Dorothy set up a grocery-cum-newsagent-cum-convenience store in Hampton Road, Twickenham. But Reg was not cut out to be a grocer — drinking, singing, playing a nifty piano, brawling and droning on about the war were apparently more in his line, or so I have been told by those who knew him. He died young, of alcoholism, in Melbourne. (My mother has never spoken a word to me about my father, other than when I was a child. Nor will she ever, I believe. All families have their secrets and tragedies; Reg Dennis is hers — and hers alone.)

I have only one memory of my father, swinging me round as a toddler in a sand pit at a Thames-side lido. I recall his moustache and slicked-back hair. But even that memory may well have been falsely implanted in my mind by a box-camera snapshot in a dusty old family album.

Reg emigrated to Australia, as so many of that post-war generation did. I was four years and three months old when he left. Neither my younger brother, Julian, nor I ever laid eyes on him again. (The plan was, apparently, that we would follow him after he'd found a job and somewhere for us to live. Julian and I were slated, then, to become immigrant kids — despised Pommy-Aussies. But it was never to be.)

Even so, I wish to record that I had a truly wonderful childhood, brought up partly by my grandmother and then by my mother, helped out pretty often by many aunts and uncles. My mother has been the defining influence on my life. Everything I have achieved I owe to her. I suspect I even gravitated towards publishing and writing because she purchased an old sit-up-and-beg Underwood typewriter when we were toddlers and deliberately left it out for my brother and me to 'hunt and peck' upon as children.

The gulf between the Middlesex infant in white sunhat and rompers feeding a milkman's horse sugar lumps (I have a photo to prove it) and the poet, entrepreneur, and planter of trees I became is immeasurable, and not just in material circumstances. The events that have made up the course of my life were described quite recently by a BBC interviewer, live on air, as 'almost beyond belief, too unlikely ever to feature in a novel.' This is maybe over-egging the custard, but not by much. I have difficulty myself believing many of the things that have happened to me in my life.

To say I was born lucky is putting it mildly. To add that I have lived more lives than one is to state the obvious. To assert that few people have had as lively a canter through modern times — financially, sexually, professionally and (unexpectedly) as a man of letters — is quite literally true. I have been laughing my way uproariously through the years (bar these last few months, naturally enough), much to the understandable irritation of many of my peers.

Let me choose a smattering of examples to support this assertion and take you on a short journey through the life and times of a very lucky man.

After an infancy in a terraced alley two up-two-down (kept scrupulously clean by my grandmother) with neither electricity, indoor lavatory, bathroom, running hot water or heating except for a coal fire, in conditions that would generate incredulity among social workers today, I find myself now living in some of the most beautiful homes on earth.

Again, I am one of the only persons alive who can truthfully say: 'I once made a chart single with John Lennon.' And how many others have had their portrait drawn by David Hockney?

Again, I met a bunch of Australians in the late 1960s in London who created one of the hippest magazines of its time. By becoming a designer, editor and business manager on this rag I was not only issued a passport to a celebrity world of London's hip and talented, I became a co-defendant in the longest conspiracy trial in British history. This put my photograph, along with my co-defendants, on the front pages of every national newspaper in the UK. Wot larx, eh? (As you might guess, my mother did not agree!)

Again, in the matter of friends, I have kept in touch with more of my friends than most. Certainly I have enjoyed their company enormously. My method was simple. I established a private office in London's West End decades ago and never permitted the telephone number to change, even when the address did. In this way, my office became a kind of 'Friends Reunited' (really 'Friends Keeping In Touch') long before the internet was invented.

And it has to be added that the generation from which those friends arose, the Baby Boomers, were perhaps the most extraordinary bunch of talented misfits since the early Victorians. Or so I believe. These friendships have acted as an enduring rock anchoring my somewhat rackety life.

Again, having dropped out of grammar school, I went on to become one of the richest self-made entrepreneurs in Britain. I still am, today. Much of this wealth resulted from my association with individuals who somehow always seemed to turn up just when I needed them. Without them, I know perfectly well (and have always known) that I could never have succeeded, either financially or professionally, to the degree that I did.

Again, early on, I decided to risk my business arm in North America. Virtually every British publishing house had attempted the same impossible dream over the decades since 1950. Virtually all failed — or would fail in due course. Instead, in New York City I met Peter Godfrey and Robert G. Bartner. They became my American partners with whom I founded many enterprises, one of which became a publicly quoted company on the NASDAQ generating two and a half billion dollars a year. Which made the three of us insufferably rich. Lucky enough? Both Peter and Bob are still close friends today.

Not to mention my establishment of *Maxim* magazine in America (against all professional advice, I might add) which, within three years of launching, was selling more magazines to young men in the US than all its rivals combined. As a result of colossal newsstand sales and our early adoption of the internet to sell subscriptions to readers, *Maxim* at its peak was probably generating more cash annually for Peter, Bob and myself than almost any other monthly magazine in the USA.

And the list goes on and on and on.

Again, like a fool, I blew over one hundred million US dollars — yes, that's $100,000,000 — on booze, drugs, ladies of easy virtue, fair-weather friends and hangers-on, clubs, partying, private jets, huge cars (despite not owning a driving licence), pointless vacations in which I sometimes booked an entire Caribbean resort, and other idiocies over which I shall discreetly draw a veil. It was fun, but not only wasted a deal of money, it also wasted my time, a far more valuable commodity. I was lucky to stop this nonsense when I did. But I cannot deny that I enjoyed the ride!

Again, as if that wasn't enough, I decided it might be fun to become a crack cocaine addict. Well, it was fun. For a short while. Then the habit began to kill me (it probably has killed me), as well as turning me, after a few years, into a partial psychotic wreck. I packed it in by eschewing all professional help or rehab and went cold turkey overnight. Difficult, but effective.

Again, I met two women in my life who truly cared for me and were (how to put this delicately?) wholly compatible with my occasionally exotic sexual requirements. It doesn't get any luckier than that, chum.

Again, I developed a passion for planting trees and founded a charity, The Heart of England Forest Ltd, to plant a large native British broadleaf forest. The project quickly attracted a dedicated team. It is situated near Stratford-upon-Avon, close to the remnants of Shakespeare's Forest of Arden. After 15 years, we have planted 2,500 acres with a million native broadleaf trees and have become the largest private planter of native trees in England, according to the Forestry Commission, (**www.heartofenglandforest.com**).

Our ideal target is to become a contiguous sunlit forest of 25,000 acres with ten million trees, wetlands, meadow pastures and areas left 'wild', always open to the general public. A forest full of light and air and controlled entirely by a charity which owns the land the trees are planted upon. A forest to last for centuries. Of course, I shall not live to see much of this, but at least the project now has a solid foundation, and I am reasonably confident, that given a few decades, it will be completed. This will be to the astonishment of an early chorus of vocal sceptics. But then, the world is full of sceptics. In my view, one should pay little attention to them.

Again, 20 years ago, I stumbled upon and bought David Bowie's house in a tiny Caribbean island called Mustique, a Windward Island in Saint Vincent and the Grenadines. Both my lover, Marie-France, and myself hugely enjoy staying on Mustique — I am writing this in a cottage there — and SVG, its people, landscape and climate have captivated us. The only governmental honour I ever accepted was to become an Honorary Consul for St Vincent. (Offered the full shabby whack in my own country as a major donor to a political party, I refused both knighthood and a seat in the House of Lords on the basis of Groucho Marx's observation: 'Who would want to belong to any club that would have me as a member?')

Again, rather late in life as these things go, I discovered I could write poetry and loved to write it. Better still, that people would buy my poetry books and come to my poetry readings in their tens of thousands. Not to mention that the Royal Shakespeare Company, with their talented actors, would perform my poetry live on both sides of the Atlantic.

Eventually, other poets and critics began to mutter flattering things about my work. They had been initially wary of taking notice of verse written by a rich entrepreneur, suspecting it might be a passing whim. A few, I am informed, swallowed a rumour that I was secretly paying a talented poet to ghost-write verse for me. Rich poets have never been popular among their peers!

Not many of us are lucky enough to discover such a talent late in life. Poetry has overtaken my existence to such a degree that I now think of myself as a poet who used to be in business — well, most of the time, anyway. To my amazement, all my books of verse are still in print and available online.

All in all, I believe I can assert that I was born unreasonably lucky, having packed in a huge amount into a shortish span — no complaints there, although I'll admit that another decade or so would have been welcome. (I can hear the Grim Reaper whispering in my ear: 'That's what they all say, mate.')

This, then, is probably the last book by me (my tenth book of poetry) that I shall know anything about. It is divided into two parts of unequal length. Book I is a small section, 'Premonitions', which includes poems written during the years when, perhaps, 'the heart knew what the mind dared not perceive', intuiting my early death. Book II is a 'Verse Diary', which contains poetry composed following my terminal diagnosis. Those that I have rejected, together with my poetry manuscripts and computer files are likely to be housed at the Bodleian Library, Oxford. All my poetry can be found, listened to and often viewed at **www. felixdennis.com**

Forgive me, gentle reader, if some of the notes under my poems are a trifle long. As a distinguished writer once observed: 'Do excuse the length of this letter. I would have shortened it, but had no time.'

Precisely.

Thank you and farewell.

Felix Dennis
Mandalay House, Mustique
January, 2014

BOOK I

'The heart knows what the mind
dares not perceive.'

SUNSET, MUSTIQUE

A ball of fire is spilling in the sea,
The empty sky flamingo-pink and grey,
Cicada songs creak out the end of day,
A choir of tree-frogs whistle: 'Come to me!'

Our feral cat is sprawled upon the wall,
The stone still warm beneath her mottled fur;
Her lantern-green eyes blink — she will not stir
Until her food is brought, nor heed my call.

I sit upon a driftwood bench and stare,
The house is full of laughter, guests and light,
I dare not stay here long, hid in the night.
The bats are out! There's one... another there!

Some fool has rung the gong. I catch my breath
And suddenly I know that I've grown old,
The courtyard cobbles, lit with bars of gold,
Spell out the hieroglyphics of a death.

Mandalay, Mustique April 24, 2004

I PLUCKED ALL THE CHERRIES

I plucked all the cherries
Chance would allow,
Take them, and welcome —
I'm done with them now.

Done with the ladder
And done with the tree,
Take them, and welcome —
They're no use to me.

Done with the getting of
What I could get,
Take it, and welcome —
Try not to forget

To pluck all the cherries
Chance will allow,
Take them, and welcome —
I'm done with them now.

Mandalay, Mustique   August 8, 2006

A BOWL OF QUINCE

While things are happening, wonderful things,
Terrible things, things we shall not forget
For as long as we live, things to regret,
To be proud of (or not!), the so-called 'slings
And arrows of...' etcetera, the scary swings
And roundabouts of living — while we fret
That doctors may not cure us or that debt
Will sink our fledgling start-up — life grows wings.
For us, the world is coming to an end,
Our bitter tears and curses dun the ears
Of gods gone deaf, our guardian angels wince
To watch us build up castles of our fears
Or tear apart a clock we cannot mend.
Meanwhile, spring came;
    a flower;
     a bee;
      this quince!

Dorsington, Warwickshire December 1, 2012

Out in the bitter cold of early December in my garden, I gathered a handful of fruit from my quince tree (just a low bush, really) and brought them inside to arrange in a bowl. All were pungent, some smooth and green, some yellow and blotched windfalls, more of a pear shape than a miniature lemon, some blackened husks rescued from leaf litter. How busy nature had been while I consumed weeks and months battling my cancer. The human sense of self all too often sets us apart from life around us, our awareness of mortality blinding us to our ultimate unimportance.

YOU CANNOT LIVE AS I HAVE LIVED

You cannot live as I have lived and not end up like this.
You cannot climb where I have climbed denying the abyss.
Long nights of iguana joys and terror on the wheel
Will lead you to a labyrinth where Minotaurs are real.

And there's the rub; for amateurs who act as if they care,
Too slow to cauterise their need to strip the wires bare:
You cannot waltz with Dracula then wave away the kiss —
You cannot live as I have lived and not end up like this.

Dorsington, Warwickshire September 12, 2007

Thanks for the first and last lines to Terence Blacker, whose biography *You Cannot Live As I Have Lived And Not End Up Like This: The thoroughly disgraceful life & times of Willie Donaldson* (Ebury Press 2007) gave me, and hopefully thousands like me, such enormous pleasure. Try this quip of Donaldson's from the book's cover blurb: 'I am someone who always answers the phone at 1 a.m. because I know it isn't going to be my bank manager or the Inland Revenue, but probably a crack dealer or a prostitute.' Donaldson will be remembered most for *The Henry Root Letters* and *Brewer's Rogues, Villains and Eccentrics*. Blacker's biography does him proud – a gem of a book.

KNOWING WHEN TO GO

Some go early — lucky them,
The eulogies are frightful;
Some expire, *cherchez* la femme,
With relatives grown spiteful.
Some go gently, two by two,
Simpatico forever,
Some cling on, like me and you,
Through any kind of weather.
Some go screaming in the dark
With demons dancing madly,
Some go witty, some go stark,
The damaged goods go gladly.
Some go sudden, swept away
Fiddling, fey, like Neros,
Some defiant, stags at bay,
The way of unsung heroes.
Some, like cats, creep out alone
To join their feral brothers.
Some are gone before they're grown
To break the hearts of mothers.
Some go vicious, some go wise,
The saddest like a robot,
The best with starlight in their eyes —
Though where they go, I know not.

Mandalay, Mustique December 23, 2001

ON NEWS OF A FRIEND'S SUDDEN DEATH
[for A-M. K. 1956 - 2001]

How thin the cloth, how fine the thread
   That cloaks the living from the dead;
How narrowly, from breath to breath,
   We plait our rendezvous with death.

How swift the tenant flees the gate;
   The landlord's writ, come soon or late,
Foreclosing slum or stately hall,
   Hard bailiffs at His beck and call.

How feather-light the feeble spark
   That shields us from the greedy dark;
Unjessed our souls like falcons fly!
   How weak the lure, how wide the sky!

Dorsington, Warwickshire   October 7, 2001

(Jesses are the leather bands attached to a trained falcon hawk's legs by the falconer. Often, a tiny bell is attached to the jess. A bird is unjessed when the band is accidentally or deliberately removed. In such circumstances, the falcon will often refuse to return to the wrist or lure and 'flies wide', never to be seen again.)

I AM LISTENING NOW

I am listening, now. The past is past,
I'm here. I'm sitting beside your bed.
Speak to me now. It's time at last
To make amends. The past is dead.

I am listening, now. I'm here, my dear.
Your spotted hands are soft as fur.
Speak to me, now. I've ears to hear,
They are not so deaf as once they were.

I am listening, now. I'm done with fuss;
Babble of treachery, love or pain,
Speak of yourself, of them, of us —
Speak of the ghosts that fill the rain.

I am listening, now. I left it late,
Later than ever we thought or knew.
Speak to me. Please. Unbar the gate.
Turn back, my dear. I'm here for you.

Mandalay, Mustique January 25, 2005

'...but the rain is full of ghosts tonight...'
— Edna St. Vincent Millay

EBB-TIDE

The tide is on the turn, its silent ebb
    Retreats before a cradled undertow,
As if a sullen spider drew its web
    Hard back within itself — and I too slow
To haul against its dark, malicious spite;
      The sea will have its due; the moon is full
        Though still invisible to earth-bound gaze,
      The waters swirl beneath its iron pull,
My feeble craft is towed, strain as I might,
And I, like Arthur, turn to face the night
        Sans hope, sans Avalon, sans minstrel lays.

Low stinking mud-flats stretch on either side
    Beyond the reach of any but the gulls,
Their screeching floats across a littered tide,
    Made perilous with hulks and scuppered hulls,
A breaker's beach of hopes beyond repair.
    But am I not myself long past the point
        Of salvaged anchors — caked in silted clay
      Hydrographers would shudder to anoint
Or mark upon a chart? Though who would care
To navigate blindfolded or by prayer?
        Beneath all copper sheathing lurks decay.

Here then we've lain to wait — abandoned wrecks
     In hidden estuaries awash with blood,
Loose cannons sprawled across the littered decks
     Of mildewed oak grown rotten with each flood.
Each yards a noose, the rudder hinged athwart,
     Each floating hell a corpse of history.
          As Death's pale mariners rise in our sleep
     To pick and choose, we cry: 'Let it be me!
Too long, too long! I've lingered in this port
Of lost despair. My battles all are fought.
          The tide is on the turn — I seek the deep!'

Mandalay, Mustique   August 11, 2013

GOING BALD

My ornamental maples are tenacious;
While oak and alder mourn for what is lost
They sulk in glory, obdurate, ungracious,
Their kamikaze boughs defying frost.

The memory of summer serenades us,
While autumn's fingers tug till we are shorn,
And winter finds us out, and death persuades us
To drop our golden hoard upon the lawn.

Dorsington, Warwickshire   April 14, 2005

THE TEST IS ALL — THE REST IS NOISE

The test is all — the rest is noise,
The music of our fears
From orchestras of floating joys —
How swift the iceberg nears!

But come the test, as steel and sea
And flesh and breath collide,
We broach redemption's mystery:
Who stands — to stand aside?

Who hoists another to the boats
To take a place they crave?
It matters not who sinks or floats —
The test is who we save.

Mandalay, Mustique January 7, 2011

Written on a day when the word 'Test' was very much in my mind, being in the grip of a debilitating bout of diarrhoea and while attempting to take my mind off the invisible giant playing double-bass with my intestines by watching England's cricket team retain the Ashes and thrash Australia by an innings in Sydney. As soon as I'd finished the poem, I realised it had come from W.E. Henley's 'Invictus' ('Out of the night that covers me...'). Henley was Robert Louis Stevenson's friend and collaborator in their youth, although they quarrelled later when RLS had established himself as by far the greater stylist and man of letters. Some say that Stevenson's greatest character in fiction, the fearsome sea cook, Long John Silver, was based on the character of the 'boisterous and piratic' Henley — himself an amputee. I do hope so. While poets like Henley (and Kipling and Stevenson, for that matter) are no longer considered quite the thing in the great cathedral of Poetry in English, anyone who discovers themselves suddenly suffering a frightening bout of sickness or depression, could do worse than turn to 'Invictus':

> It matters not how strait the gate,
>   How charged with punishment the scroll,
> I am the master of my fate:
>   I am the captain of my soul.

THE DIAGNOSIS
[To Dr. M.B. & Dr. M.M.]

Patronising waffle,
Yet another test,
Traipsing through the clinic,
Stripping off my vest.
Answering their questions,
Breathing in and out,
Watching other patients
Wandering about.
Reeling off my symptoms,
Trying hard to pee,
Cursing hypodermics,
Dreading the big 'C'.
Fumbling with buttons,
Dying for a beer,
Begging the Almighty
'Get me out of here!'
Sneering at the muzak,
Leering at the nurse,
Standing for the X-rays,
Wondering which is worse —

Knowing, or not knowing.
Guzzling orangeade,
Tranquillised and dozing:
Growing more afraid.
Woken in a tizzy,
Stumbling down the hall:
'Delighted to inform you...
...nothing wrong at all.'
Glory *Hallelujah*!
Babbling in relief;
Straight off down the boozer:
'What's your poison, chief?'

Mandalay, Mustique January 18, 2001

Back in September 1999, I thought I was dying. The symptoms were scary. Bloated, lethargic and barely able to walk in a straight line or lift my limbs, I set off on a weary round of tests in London's Harley Street under the care of Dr. Milton Maltz. Ultrasound tests, X-rays, CAT scans, urine and blood tests, bone examinations — all revealed nothing. Finally, I was diagnosed by a thyroid specialist (it took him less than a minute!) as hypothyroidatic. A little white pill a day and in one week I was a new man. The magic of science!

LIFE SUPPORT

Upon a bed of ice and fire,
   I waited, swathed in tube and wire,
      My lungs a searing funeral pyre:
         They asked me my religion — I was dying.
Grown weary in the fever's grip
   I watched an intravenous drip
      Pump ballast, then abandoned ship;
         'He's sinking!' cried a nurse. I thought: *I'm flying!*

Much later, while I convalesced
   I learned what I'd already guessed,
      When on his rounds, a quack confessed:
         'We nearly lost you, son. You just weren't trying.
I've seen it once or twice before...
   You wandered through an open door
      But can't remember what you saw?'
         'You're right,' I said. And found that I was crying.

Mandalay, Mustique July 4, 2001

With sincere thanks to the doctors, nurses and diagnosticians of Danbury Hospital, Connecticut, who (not to put too fine a point on it) saved my life in September 1988.

IN A CEMETERY

What is a headstone but a bolted door
That opens once, then slams to seal in earth
The cast-off, decomposing cloak we wore?

A door on which is scratched a date of birth
And death; perhaps our former occupation;
Fine words in all sincerity or mirth;

A line of poetry or some quotation
To emphasise the late-departed's worth —
Which, true or not, is twaddle in translation.

There's nothing here to worship or adore,
To contemplate or fear — the transformation
Is purely chemical and nothing more.

Tomorrow's flowers are seeds among the weeds
We sow today: the past knows nought of needs.

New York City   April 19, 2013

Written the day after hearing that a young ex-employee at my private office, Luke Short, had
died unexpectedly. In my mind, I wandered into an imaginary cemetery, wondering what I
would inscribe on Luke's headstone. Then I realised it didn't matter what I, or anyone else,
inscribed. He was what he was. The tragedy of his death is what it is. Some hurts are never
healed. For those who love poetics, this is a sonnet whose form I believe I have invented,
or re-invented perhaps. The aba, bcb, cbc, aca, dd rhyme scheme is an attempt to echo the
pointless circularity of living and dying, while the three line stanza four-use rhyme form,
melded into an 'English' sonnet structure, is one I've never seen used before — as far as my
memory serves me.

MY FIRST THOUGHT WAS

My first thought was of Browning's evil hour,
That hoary cripple's psychopathic ruse;
Now all pretence is gone, then I must choose:
A ditch in which to die — or storm the tower,
Blind to wanton purpose or its power,
My coat-of-mail this faithless, fleeting Muse.

Fine sentiments! But scant reality
Grants less than miracles — those loaves and fish
That once fed multitudes a fabled dish
Grow thin upon the ground near famine's tree:
'Dear God, can this be happening to me?'
Why should it not since Eve was taught to wish?

And taught by one who slithers even now
For those who still believe — though as for that
I have no more belief than my old cat
Waiting contentedly, a worn-out plough
Who scarcely breaks her purrs with her meow
While cancer chews her bowels upon the mat.

My next thought was: I have so little time...

Mandalay, Mustique May 13, 2013

In fact, this was written at Dorsington in May of last year when I suspected I was not going to survive my bout with throat cancer. Then I mislaid the draft lines and only discovered them again a year later (almost to the day) here in Mustique. I wrote a fourth stanza today:

My last thought was: I have so little time

To write, to think, to blubber or to choose

A likely tyke whose feet might fill my shoes

In his or her own way —

which referred to the fulfilment of planting 25,000 acres for The Heart of England Forest; but my heart wasn't in it and the rawness of the original three stanzas must serve. The reference, of course, is to Robert Browning's mighty ballad: 'Childe Roland to the Dark Tower Came'. If you've not read it, please search it out; I promise you, you're in for a treat! My old cat is now buried in my orchard; Moushka was my companion, on and off, for nearly 17 years.

I AM FLEEING FOR MY LIFE

I am fleeing for my life — or maybe from it —
'The thief doth fear each bush an officer',
The years have seared the stars since Halley's comet
And neither speed nor wind are what they were
When adolescent lungs were near immortal,
When muscle, flesh and bone were knitted steel:
I am fleeing for my life, though through which portal
I little know or care — nor which is 'real'.

I am emptying the wine from life's decanter —
While musing, 'Do I dare?' each glass I pour;
I have grown too fond of gallows-haunted banter,
Nor am I quite as knowing as before,
For the laughter of the gods grows ever louder
And I mark the rents through which their weary eyes
Peer down upon this world of paint and powder,
Where nothing is as kind as it is wise.

I am learning to wear purple and surround it
With rhyme-edged braid to urge the world to waltz:
Should I leave it one whit better than I found it,
What of it, when all scenery is false?
I have planted out a forest — who shall ward it
Through storm, through blast, shall owe no debt to me:
I am fleeing for my life — or else toward it —
And little know or care which one it be.

Dorsington, Warwickshire   March 29, 2009

Suspicion always haunts the guilty mind;
The thief doth think each bush an officer.
— William Shakespeare Henry VI, Pt 3

    And indeed there will be time
To wonder, 'Do I dare?' and, 'Do I dare?'
Time to turn back and descend the stair...
    — from 'The Love Song of J. Alfred Prufrock' by T. S. Eliot

When I am an old woman I shall wear purple
With a red hat which doesn't go, and doesn't suit me.
    — from 'Warning' by Jenny Joseph

FOR THOSE WHO KNEW — IT WASN'T TRUE

For those who knew—it wasn't true,
No matter if they wanted to,
Who kicked and fumed against the pricks
Of bearded rogues—the dirty tricks
Of costumed ranters casting stones
While venerating piles of bones,
And fetching wood to burn old crones...

For those who stood against the fear
Or those that ran, but held the rear,
Who fought a creeping worm of shame,
Who sought no other fool to blame,
Who read the books and thought 'em through
And wanted to believe, but knew
Most likely, that it wasn't true...

For those who snuffed the candle out
To wander, lost, in caves of doubt,
Who faced what they each knew must come,
Who flinched, and yet would not succumb
To blandishments or threats; their cry:
'You preach that heretics must die,
If what you say is true— then <u>why</u>?

Men's gods are born of Man's own dread,
A dread that seeks its own twin dead,
And as faith waned, your hatred grew
For those who know—it isn't true.'

Mandalay, Mustique   March 24, 2007

FAITH AND HOPE

Faith is armoured, girt for war,
Certain of one creed, one law.
Hope stands naked — and unsure.

Faith seeks sinners to retrieve,
Flaying those that disbelieve.
Hope seems helpless — and naive.

Yet the brightest steel may rust,
Faithless gods return to dust.
Hope outlives all things — in trust.

Dorsington, Warwickshire   May 8, 2011

I FEAR THE WIND

I fear the wind — I always did,
Its scudding tides of dread and doubt;
And as a child, wherever I hid,
The wind would always find me out.

I feared the crocodile sob of air,
The shriek of tortured trees outside;
'The Devil's abroad in coach and pair,'
My Nan would sniff, *'no use to hide.'*

But I fear the wind, it's eerie tongue,
The clatter of nameless things in flight —
For I have known, since I was young,
That I shall die on a stormy night.

Mandalay, Mustique   February 21, 2005

ALONE

Always, always, we are alone.
The solitude of self prevails
For worker bee or cast out drone,
In palaces, on beds of nails,
Worshipped as a new messiah,
Shunned as neighbourhood pariah,
Proud or fearful — on our own.

Always, always, we are alone.
Though our lover loves us madly
We are but a house of bone,
Skin and bone they'd die for gladly;
Sunk in cells of stony quiet,
Whirled in carnival or riot,
Dead or living — on our own.

Always, always, we are alone,
Flushed with triumph, broken-hearted,
Old and knowing, scarcely grown,
Blighted by the griefs we've charted,
Innocents abroad or traitors,
Bankers, beggars, proud dictators,
Come the reckoning — on our own.

Dorsington, Warwickshire June 30, 2012

Inspired by 'The Solitude of Self', an impassioned speech delivered by Elizabeth Cady
Stanton to the Judiciary Committee of the US House of Representatives on January 17th
1892, in favour of a 16th amendment and the rights of women in America.

FORGET-ME-NOTS

And is there resurrection for the wave
Breaking its arced heart on imperious stone,
Or for the common or garden trilling
Of April blackbirds, squandering their lone
Mellifluous rills on an empty sky?
Men are not the only ones who die.

Or a heavenly house for the lost chords
Of storm-lashed rigging, or the fogbound horn
Of ships on a lee shore, or a scrapbook
Enshrining their perfection on the first dawn
The pyramids of Giza split the sky?
Men are not the only things that die.

Is there redemption for the loyalties
Of dogs, or for sculpted crusts of permafrost,
For mutant spores bred in laboratories?
The truth is — no. The truth is, all is lost;
Lost in forget-me-nots of wind and sky.
Men are not the only ones who die.

Soho, London   April 5, 2005

IN FLIGHT
After a Cancer Scare, flying from Mustique to Britain

So it begins — the last descent, long feared
Though long expected. Here then, in this pause,
Let me take stock, as if an angel peered
Upon my soul's mute rage and dull applause.

Come seek then, spectral dunce, survey the void
Of one who never sought or bought your aid.
Should all I wrought or fought for be destroyed
Can what is lost be less than what was made?

Omnipotent? Perhaps — yet I suspect
That time has naught to fear from men or gods —
The sham of cause is equal to effect
And Einstein's dice obey no law or odds.

Rambling fool! Bravado builds no boats
Nor plies an oar to swim some trackless mere;
Who sorts iambic herders from their goats
With hounds of hell upon the heels of fear?

Let us be calm. At forty-thousand feet,
Within this gilded bird's unholy pride,
No word has yet been spoken of defeat:
If loathsome Death may stalk, may Hope not hide?

And so it begins, the long descent to — where?
This flight from Paradise to homely hell
Is buoyed by more than wings, but less than prayer,
Too high to hear the tolling of a bell.

40,000 ft above the Atlantic January 16, 2012

I SHALL NEVER BE YOUNG AGAIN

(S.D. the first of my friends to die)

I shall never be young again
In deed or word, by speech or pen,
Though feckless grief may soon desert
Its post and time shall heal my hurt,
And pat my back and send me hence —
The gift of what was innocence
Is lost, nor can it be restored.
Fate has shown the thing a fraud.

My life, 'til now, an unalloyed
Mad Hatter's Ball, confronts the void,
Those gods I thought my bosom friends
Have demonstrated who depends
On who — 'No use to stammer why
Or when', they cry — 'you live, you die,
Forgotten even as you leave.
Your lives were dreams of make-believe.'

I kissed her brow. So cold! Since then,
I have never been young again.

Mandalay, Mustique August 4, 2013

MEN DIE LIKE FLIES

Men die like flies — as they have ever done,
    And all our chaff of immortality
    Is gloss and glaze on Death's reality,
The plated silverware of races run.
What's done is done — and we are all undone,
    Our cruelty, our kindnesses and vanity,
    Our cowardice and talents and urbanity,
The love we swore would long outlive the sun.
Donne's 'Mighty and dreadful... thou art not so,'
    Rings subtly false, if noble in its power,
    And yet I think though men may beg and cower
Beneath the certainty of Death's last blow,
    Still, to have lived in wonder, hour by hour,
Is recompense suffice for mortal woe.

Mandalay, Mustique   January 7, 2012

This sonnet was completed just a week before I was diagnosed with the Big 'C', a somewhat odd coincidence. Would I have changed it had I known then what I know now? Yes! And I *did* change it, but only the Bodleian Library at Oxford (which is curating my poetry manuscripts, digital files and papers) will be able to decipher the original from this printed version. There's a lot less bravado in it now!

Death, be not proud, though some have callèd thee
    Mighty and dreadful, for thou art not so;
    For those whom thou think'st thou dost overthrow
Die not, poor Death, nor yet canst thou kill me.
    — John Donne (1572 - 1631) 'Holy Sonnets'

RUTLAND BAY

The end of the world round here is Rutland Bay,
White spume engulfs the cliffs with weed and spray,
Jurassic frigate birds, white gulls in tow,
Drag shadows over salt pond scrub below.

Along this beach of cast-off trash and stone
Among the flotsam wrack, I slouch alone,
And stop, and stare, and think of waves that churn
A different sea — from which no ships return.

Mandalay, Mustique May 12, 2013

Although always windy (yes, *always*, even when the rest of the island is breathless with dead air) and somewhat forlorn with its salt ponds, scrub, wild grass and cacti, shingle, stones, boulders, flotsam and jetsam, cast off materials from small boats and yachts and fishermen — despite all this Rutland Bay is a magnet for those who wish to be alone. The crashing waves, scrape of shingle and the ever-present wind make it hard to hold a conversation, even with yourself! We have wilder landscapes on Mustique (North Point comes to mind, which resembles a moonscape) but for lonesome melancholy, Rutland Bay takes the biscuit.

10/10/10
For J StCB, PCE, FT, GK, CT, JC, AS, JD, PL, SM

Preposterous — I know it to be so.
A glorious day, gold leaves beneath my feet,
The sun upon my back, tall trees aglow
With autumn's alchemy; the soft air sweet,
The wind the merest whisper in my ears,
A church bell's chimes, the thrushes on the wing
And all is as it should be, save these tears —
As rootless as the source from which they spring.
I am a hard man, save when I write, perhaps,
Despising showy grief — '*I did not die,*
I am not here.' — false sentiment that wraps
The hardest truth we learn within a lie.
    But ten in fifty weeks; lives ripped to dross.
    And now this ugly date to mock our loss.

Dorsington, Warwickshire October 10, 2010

WE ARE ALL BEDE'S BIRD

We are all Bede's bird.
Darting into a hall of light
One frozen, solitary night
To find to our astonishment
A world of warmth, of wonderment,
Awash with sounds that shake our frame
And things for which we have no name,
Our flight too fast to bank or stall,
We sheer across the feasting hall
And out into the frozen sky,
Some say to live, some say to die,
(And some that we've not flown at all,
But simply dreamt up feast and hall...)
Though all agree, once out the door
The sparrow may return no more —
It seems absurd, but I have heard
Brave men have died to pass The Word
That we are all Bede's bird.

Dorsington, Warwickshire July 5, 2011

'Such,' he said, 'O King, seems to me the present life of men on earth, in comparison with that time which to us is uncertain, as if when on a winter's night you sit feasting with your earldormen and brumali, and a simple sparrow should fly into the hall, and coming in at one door, instantly fly out through another. In that time in which it is indoors it is indeed not touched by the fury of the winter; but yet, this smallest space of calmness being passed almost in a flash, from winter going into winter again, it is lost to our eyes. Somewhat like this appears the life of man, but of what follows or what went before, we are utterly ignorant.' — The Venerable Bede *Ecclesiastical History*, Book II, 731 a.d. The story of the consultation between Edwin of Northumbria and his nobles whether they shall accept the missionary gospel as preached by Paulinus.

A PHOTO ALBUM OF VICTORIAN LONDON

A book of London, long ago —
The roads awash with shit and snow,
Street Arabs at a chestnut stall,
Pinched faces in the brazier's glow.

A feral cat upon a wall,
An apple-seller's sheep-shank shawl,
Slumped horses, thin and underfed,
Wet cobbles glistening in a squall.

Pert missy with a loaf of bread,
Her bonnet flounced about her head,
A beau's arm crooked to lean upon;
Dark alleys only thieves would tread.

All dead, all dead. All dead and gone,
Where once a shuttered lens had shone,
The marvel is that life goes on,
The marvel is that life goes on.

Mandalay, Mustique   August 21, 2013

THIS IS THE SONG

This is the song that none can sing,
This is the gift the old gods bring,
Sung this once as the soul takes wing
In the emptiness of night.

Here is the powerlessness of speech,
The letting go that none can teach,
The song of things beyond our reach
Singing to its own light.

Mandalay, Mustique April 9, 2007

LONE WOLF

Loping down a muddy track —
Rabid — toothless — fled the pack —
Vegan wolf — no appetite —
Lost the bark — mislaid the bite.

Outcast — loopy — pelt gone grey —
Loner — turncoat — hunts no prey —
Scavenger — laps verse for blood —
Drowning in an autumn flood.

Dorsington, Warwickshire September 6, 2002

WHAT DO WE OWE THE DEAD?

What do we owe the dead
  When leaden night has claimed them,
When flesh and word have fled,
  And memory has framed them?
      To speak no ill,
      To shield them still,
    To veil their misdemeanours
      From disrepute,
      To substitute
    Chihuahuas for hyenas?
What do we owe the dead
  When flame or dust has claimed them,
When all excuse is fled
  And martyr's light has framed them?

What do we owe to whom,
  Their kin — their friends — their lovers?
Shall history presume
  That truth must trump all others —
    No stone unturned,
    No diary burned,
    No papers left encoded,
    No kindly vault
    To shutter fault —
    No smoking gun unloaded?
What do we owe the dead
  When those in trust have shamed them,
When all excuse is fled,
  And tribe or scribe has claimed them?

Dorsington, Warwickshire July 5, 2011

The metre and rhyme-scheme for this poem comes from 'Oft In The Stilly Night' by
Thomas Moore (1779 - 1852). The son of a Dublin grocer, Moore became a successful poet and
singer, known chiefly for his 'Poems', published in 1801, and his even more successful 'Irish
Melodies'. Lord Byron entrusted his unpublished 'Memoirs' to Moore with instructions to
publish it following his (Byron's) death. After first selling the manuscript to a bookseller for
2,000 guineas, Moore had second thoughts and borrowed a small fortune to reclaim it. He
then claimed to have burnt the manuscript. Not all literary sleuths are convinced he did so
and harbour hopes that one day this sensational document may come to light. It was the
apparent breach of trust by Moore which suggested the title and theme of this poem to me.
Undoubtedly, he did what he did to protect the reputation of his friend. What, indeed, do
we owe the dead?

THREE THINGS

Three things, perhaps, will haunt me at the last:
   The doors I left unopened as I passed;
The shade of seeds I nurtured in the ground;
   The heartache of a love I never found.

Mandalay, Mustique January 16, 2009

THE RILL OF HOPE

What feeds this feeble rill of Hope
Trickling to a lake of Doubt?
Whose servants march beside its slope
Whispering of dams and drought?

From beck to brook, from brook to stream,
To cataracts of roiling grief
Which thunder through a fevered dream
To drown in pools of disbelief...

What nourishment from depthless wells —
From sunless seas — what nameless source
Dares circumscribe our private hells
To bid our helmsman: 'Hold your course!'

When all is lost, when terror reigns
And men despair; when deaths are cures
And rope the remedy for pains:
Still, drop by drop, Hope's rill endures!

Dorsington, Warwickshire January 31, 2012

This is another poem written shortly after the confirmation of the diagnosis of my throat cancer back in January 2012. I like Leonard Cohen's take on the subject. He once quipped: 'Sure, there is a crack in everything. That's how the light gets in.'

WHISPERED THE ROWAN TO THE OAK

The woods of our youth are failing,
   even the mightiest rot,
Beetle and high wind take them
   and soon they will be forgot,
Yet sadder than even the fading
   of suns too eager to set
Is that you should fail to remember
   what I can never forget.

Saplings of strangers surround us
   to feather the winter sky,
Yet though you survive beside me,
   you see with an empty eye,
Far better we fall and nourish
   the land in a last duet
Than that you should fail to remember
   what I can never forget.

Mandalay, Mustique January 1, 2007

I CANNOT DO THIS WITHOUT YOU

I cannot do this without you. Yet I cannot ask.
You must choose to see — or choose not to look about you.
The book of our lives is closing, closing. This last task,
This wretched thing, remains. I cannot do this without you.

Dorsington, Warwickshire June 10, 2009

SUNSET, MID-JULY

Sunset, mid-July — the failing light
Salutes a sway-backed cedar on the lawn
And liquefies the words I thought to write:
Not all nights are followed by a dawn,

And not all hurts can ever be put right.
The glory of the world, which sick men mourn
As life leaks out of them, remains as bright
As on the day each living thing was born.

Nor can we stem the tide of coming night —
No man, no cedar, oak or ash or thorn.
Not all hurts can ever be put right,
And not all nights are followed by a dawn.

Dorsington, Warwickshire July 14, 2006

ENVOI!

The light is failing even as I speak,
I turn to face the last flush of the sun,
The hawser grows more frayed, the mast more weak,
And of my fleet, all ships have sailed but one.

Mandalay, Mustique   July 30, 2007

ADIEU!

Chance makes brothers but hearts make friends,
Here then, before our friendship ends
As now it must, my friend, be glad
For what we shared — for what we had.

How late we learned, how little we knew
Of those who stood, blade-straight, steel-true,
To brace when push had come to shove:
Chance makes brothers — but hearts make love!

Candlewood Lake, Connecticut   October 23, 2012

NOT ALL THINGS GO WRONG

Not all things go wrong, and knowing
    This, be wary of despair,
As you go through hell — keep going,
    Make no brave oasis there.

Through the shadowlands of grieving,
    Past the giants, Doubt and Fear,
Heartsick, stunned, and half believing —
    Heed no whisper in your ear.

Not all things go wrong — and after
    Winter's famine comes the spring,
Kindness, beauty, children's laughter —
    Joy is ever on the wing.

Mandalay, Mustique January 10, 2008

EPITAPH
To be carved on a rock on a hill in Dorsington Wood

Felix Dennis
(1947 - 2 - - -)
Poet • Publisher • Planter of Trees
'Everything. All the time.'

My friends were true,
  much love was mine,
We toasted life
  in verse and wine,
With chance my guide
  earth's wealth I knew,
And now my trees
  seed dreams anew.

Dorsington, Warwickshire October 8, 2013

BOOK II

'Come in No.9. Your time is up.'

TOO MUCH IS GOING RIGHT

Too much is going right, and being a Brit
Of a certain sort, I know I'll have to pay
At some point down the road. From where I sit
I'm riding for a fall — big time, too, I'd say.

Mock all you want, but Fate has a certain way
Of equalling the odds with Fortune's writ,
While none but a fool would balk at making hay
In summer sun, the books are cooked to fit.

The hags of Providence have little wit,
Their melancholy looms weave shades of grey
As chaos slits the cloth and all is lit
With dazzling rainbow hues, soon shut away.

Take it from me, too much good luck soon fades,
We'll only have to pay it back — in spades.

Dorsington, Warwickshire September 30, 2013

A SHADOW ON MY LUNG

'There's a shadow on my lung.'
'Uh-huh. So what?'
'It might be cancer.'
'Maybe. Maybe not.'
'And if it is, I'll die.'
'Perhaps. You might.'
'You don't seem too perturbed.'
'You've got that right.'
'I'm speaking here of death.'
'A waking dream.'
'I thought the dream was life?'
'So it might seem.'
'So which is which, my friend?'
'Why spoil the plot?'
'I'm speaking here of death.'
'Uh-huh. So what?'

Dorsington, Warwickshire September 30, 2013

TERMINAL
(Author to self the day after the final diagnosis)

When the hugging and the 'anything I can do...'
Has shut the door so that you find yourself alone
Confronting a silent chorus — knowing it's true —
With rehearsals of an untimely death: your own,
Mindlessly chanting a vulgar nursery rhyme:
'You are going to die. You are going to die...'
When you are left — bereft — to calculate your time,
Too paralysed and cowed by fear even to try,
Even to begin to try, to negotiate
With non existent entities your pair of twos
Against the royal running flush of careless Fate,
Take what breath you can in traitorous lungs, and choose:
    To spend whatever time is left in terror's grip,
    Or laugh and *live* before you give this world the slip.

Dorsington, Warwickshire   October 2, 2013

THE NIGHTS ARE DRAWING IN

The nights are drawing in, as is my life.
What could be more natural? Why then do I plead
For time, more time, when all time brings is strife;
For books I own but now shall never read;
For foreign lands whose shores I shall not tread;
For strangers who were destined to be friends;
For shaggy coats, soft purrs, ducks gobbling bread,
For shining water where the river bends?
My dearest friends, I've lived more lives than one
And lived them all at joyous, jostling speed;
My foes, if such there be: the race is run,
Come, here's my hand — forgive the word or deed.
    My loves, (and there were many, I confess),
    I bid you love as well again. God bless!

Dorsington, Warwickshire   October 7, 2013

GOOD POET, BAD POET, DEAD POET

The ice is there —
It has to be to write;
A legislating sliver in the heart,

Obliged to share
A vent of irksome light,
A dart to spark the fire of passion's art.

Words, to be sure,
Are nothing to the ice,
Our hieroglyphics neither burn nor grieve,

Sublime, piss-poor,
We pay a poet's price:
And end as we began — dead men on leave.

Dorsington, Warwickshire   October 8, 2013

'Poets are the unacknowledged legislators of the world.'
  — Percy Bysshe Shelley, 'A Defence of Poetry' (1812)

'We Communists are all dead men on leave.'
  Eugen Leviné's speech to the Court in June 1919 at his trial for high
  treason in Munich. He was found guilty and executed by firing squad.

'SEIZE THE FISH!'

There are no second acts, except in plays.
With intervals for unexpected deaths —
Or births — or marriages. The slayer slays
Because he can. Between habitual breaths
What rhyme is there, what reasons for his cunning?
Except the urge that leads us to conceive?
And what of us? We run to keep on running
Too often to postpone a time to grieve.
Dear, take my hand and stare into my eyes —
The pebbles there have long abandoned tears;
My love is such, I loathe to feed to you lies:
Our doom demands we face our greatest fears.
    I have a friend whose motto 'Seize the fish!'
    Would serve as well as Plato's dismal dish.

Dorsington, Warwickshire October 11, 2013

'Carpe diem' — Horace '*Odes*'
Commonly translated as 'Seize the day!', the full thought is: 'Carpe diem, quam minimum credula postero', or 'Enjoy today, trusting little in tomorrow.' My friend, Don Atyeo's habitual, jocular toast, 'Seize The Fish!' when wine is poured, insists on deliberately muddling the Latin phrase, substituting 'carpe' which means 'to seize', for the bottom-dwelling family of fish called 'carp' in English.

Dismal dish? 'Now it is time we were going, I to die and you to live, but which of us has the happier prospect is unknown to anyone but God.' — Plato '*Apology*' trans. H. Tredennick.

A MAPLE LEAF

The leaf had blown for half a field
    To land beyond my hedge,
I crossed the lawn to pluck its stem
    And trace its ragged edge.

Its time was up, its fate long sealed:
    To shred in winter's freeze.
I bore it back beneath its bough —
    More humus means more trees!

Dorsington, Warwickshire   October 11, 2013

DESPAIR

I am writing two letters I know I'll destroy
  I am fashioning purposeless lists,
Grown wise at the feintings our scruples deploy
  To keep us from slitting our wrists.

I am fondling objects that soon I shall lose,
  And dusting off books on their shelves,
I am haunting the hedgerows and sharing my news
  With creatures more wise than ourselves.

I am reckoning assets, (such things must be done),
  And planning the best for the worst,
If my wishes were horses, I'd choose just the one —
  To bear off my mother's life first.

I am heart-sick for lovers, for friends who will mourn,
  I have given my dog to a friend,
I am bracing to bear what I know must be borne,
  Though I fear I shall break at the end.

Dorsington, Warwickshire October 12, 2013

Oddly, this was written on a morning when it rained a little, then the sun broke through and the clouds vied with blue sky all day. I had had an absolutely magical reception from a Liverpool audience at my poetry reading the night before — almost as if they sensed they would never see me again. I believe we sold more of my poetry books afterwards than at any previous event. I should have been in reasonable shape after a night sleeping in bed (I often just doze in a chair) without any artificial aid. But it was not to be. Despair overwhelmed me. Prior knowledge of one's imminent death is a fearful burden — who to tell? How to accommodate oneself to such an alien notion? What to do or not to do concerning those left behind? We must all die sooner or later, of course; but pray you get hit by a bus or keel over with a massive coronary, or fall off a cliff or whatever... knowledge that you have weeks or months to live and that the end will likely be a rotten one is not the way I would choose. It's not just the despair and fear, it's the endless lying to those around you whom you wish to shelter from the burden of knowing for as long as you can. But hey — we don't get what we want or what we deserve in this life. We get what we get. And I guess we must be grateful for that, no matter how it ends. (Oh, I left the two letters undestroyed in the safe. My companion and best friend must make of them what they can. They, at least, will forgive me my trespasses.)

TO ONE I MIGHT HAVE MARRIED

I write to one whom I had put aside.
To one I knew.
The gods themselves, grown jealous had applied
Their poisonous dew;

But all the blame was mine, not pagan choirs.
My selfish wit
Conspired to spurn the one pledge love requires:
Commit! Commit!

Excuses, broken home — hot loins — life's brew
Were pride's sick jest;
Men thought me a success — yet we both knew
I failed the test.

Dorsington, Warwickshire October 20, 2013

THIS DYING LARK'S ALL RIGHT

This dying lark's all right —
Apart from the oblivion bit.
The will sworn and the end in sight.

The sleeping pills at night,
And bowls of bran to keep you fit.
This dying lark's all right.

The blubbering's no delight —
There's more than one wrist I could slit —
But the will's sworn; the end's in sight.

My memories veer and flit
While making notes for my obit.
This dying lark's all right.

I gave the aunt a fright
With cock-and-bull of a bastard chit
Slapped in the will with the end in sight.

Of course I'm scared, bone white.
I curse my luck when I'm down; but shit,
This dying lark's all right.
The will sworn and the end in sight.

Dorsington, Warwickshire October 20, 2013

In the immortal words of Rudyard Kipling: 'You're a better man than I am, Gunga Din.'

'The will sworn...' There has been more bureaucracy shoved under my nose this last 20 days than in the last 20 years. Dying in Britain provides endless fees, salaries, and pension contributions for 'professionals' both in and out of government. And I am told there is a lot more to come.

MY LOVE IS ALL DARK MATTER

My love is all Dark Matter, pierced and creased
With what that rascal Newton held in store —
This all-devouring universe — and more.
A ring-thane's hall where warriors rut and feast.
What's first is last in love. What's more is least.
Yet knowing nothing of what love is for
Or what may crouch and creep within its core,
I hesitate to loose or feed the beast.
A lover's hand creeps into yours, and yet
Where lies the well, the spring, the streams that set
Your pea-green pilgrim's boat upon its course?
What force could trample or obliterate
The maps before you met to wipe life's slate?
Our love is all Dark Matter at its source.

Soho, London   October 24, 2013

This sonnet was begun after I had brought myself to tell my long-time American lover, Suzen Murakoshi, that I was dying. This was not an easy thing to do. After she had been persuaded to fly back to New York City, I left the first two lines unfinished and began an exhausting ten hour stint putting together a (hopefully) workable plan for the management of my companies on my death — followed by a two hour formal Board meeting to approve those complex plans and to promote new directors to the Board. Finally, after everyone had left, I fell into an exhausted sleep in front of the fire in my Soho flat where I have lived for 40 years and which is directly above my private office in Central London. Waking at about four in the morning, I walked, clear headed and almost lightheartedly into my study, opened the door to my flower-boxed roof garden to let in the night air, and began work on my trusty old Macintosh Cube desktop computer. Within an hour or so it was done. Four small points: humankind will never get to the bottom of Dark Matter, which we currently believe makes up more than 90% of our universe; just as scientists discarded the theory of ether, they will discard Dark Matter and attempt some other attack on coming to grips with the source and substance of what is all around us. Secondly, I truly believe that men will learn to travel faster than the speed of light, which will open the gate for us to begin to populate first the solar system and then galaxies far beyond it. Thirdly, a thane was a lord, usually a warrior chief, in Anglo-Saxon times who often kept the loyalty of his followers by offering them valuable silver and gold rings, torques or arm bands. Lastly, the pea-green boat, of course, was the one those odd lovers The Owl and the Pussy-Cat chose to go to sea in as described so lovingly by the inestimable, (dare I say 'runcible'?), Edward Lear.

AUTUMN LEAVES

Piled up against the garden gate
These leaves know nothing of their fate,
Bright scarlet, cream or golden-eyed,
They neither ken nor care they've died.

And of the seven months they grew
No bud, no vein, no leaflet knew
The wonders of their chemistry,
Nor preached their secret ministry —

To cleanse, to stem as shield and crutch,
Would that Men could claim as much,
Now I shall rake these ash and oak
And poplar leaves to holy smoke.

Dorsington, Warwickshire   October 26, 2013

If one must bear the imminent knowledge of one's own death (and I suspect few would lightly choose that option), then autumn is the time to learn. All around in the English countryside the annual circle of life and death is at its most brazen as leaves litter the ground, seeds set and grasses, weeds and pond algae wither. Dead winter is in prospect. Will one be able to make it through the long huddled nights into a burgeoning spring? Will one ever see leaves back on the broadleaf trees, house martins scooping up mud for their nests, or hear the gardeners complaining again that it's time to recondition the mowers? It would be nice to think so, but only time and the daemon on my left shoulder can know for certain. And as time is neither sentient nor self-aware and the daemon a long-standing figment of my imagination... ah well: 'In nature there are no rewards or punishments; only consequences.'

COULD I HAVE DONE MUCH BETTER?

Could I have done much better?
 I don't doubt that I could.
For example — in more kindliness,
 That decoy flight to good.

But could I have tried harder?
 No — and I'll tell you why,
My aim was flawed, but then again,
 The rate of fire was high.

Indeed, too high, too passionate
 For lover, friend or foe,
A selfish hail to weave a veil
 Behind which none might go.

Should I have been more moderate
 Or scaled the scholar's scree?
Perhaps I could've, should've, might...
 But would I have stayed me?

I made the road by walking it,
 Not as a scholar strives,
There are no giant's backs to climb
 In Soho bars and dives.

And did I care to learn to care?
    And should I have, back then?
My dad had loaded wings with death
    To murder other men.

When families were damaged goods,
    Disguising their despair
As uncles slurred: 'Bear up, old man,'
    Who dared to learn to care?

And what of those things spiritual
    Which languished in disuse?
Were all my songs in Darwin's praise
    Convenient excuse?

And might I have reached out a hand
    More often than I did?
We're back to kindliness, I think,
    That upturned pyramid...

And may I now 'forgive' myself —
    The quest, the beast in view,
The inner child unreconciled?
    Dear Christ —
        I wish I knew!

Dorsington, Warwickshire October 27, 2013

TO DON

Our ties will never fray nor bend,
Now you must live for me — to lend
Your joys and revels til the end:
Live long, laugh much, love well. I send
My love;
      live for me, too, my friend.

Dorsington, Warks October 26, 2013

TO PEBWORTH

When last I walked to Pebworth,
The hedges white with May,
New lambs played king-o-the-castle,
The Downs in emerald lay.

I paused to root a bush out —
Beside a hedge close by,
Hedge-murderers these blackberries,
They smother, then they die.

I passed Hill House — the farmer
Was laughing as we met,
'You're less of a townie now, boy,
You'll make a farmer yet!'

When next I walk to Pebworth,
The hedges white with snow,
No mortal eye shall see me pass —
So softly I shall go.

Mandalay, Mustique   April 3, 2014

GRAVE GOODS

Six men with straps, the muddy clay pit damp
With last night's rain, the wicker coffin strewn
With flowers, loaded dice, a nipple clamp,
A tot of bourbon, healing crystal, Moon-
-on-her-back club ashtray, two manuscripts
In plastic folders — God knows of what ilk —
(What light is there to read in graves or crypts?)
A book of poems wrapped in violet silk,
The inevitable lock of hair in a locket,
And thoroughly invisible to mourning eyes
Something secret slipped inside his pocket —
I'd placed it there; a gift his gods would prize.
    A nod and twelve strong arms decanting bone,
    Tears and Nick's sweet dirge on saxophone.

Dorsington, Warwickshire November 3, 2013

This occasion was the burial of my old chum Michael Farren on September 19, 2013 in Dorsington Wood, Warwickshire. The reception was a gathering of the tribes, from literary scholars to Hells Angels giants, musicians and artists, sad-eyed ladies of the lowlands and DNA cowboys. Mick was a strange, difficult, contrary and altogether wonderful, talented man. In his will, he left me his silver-topped Dr. John walking cane. Here is the inscription on his studded belt-buckle bronze marker in the wood:

MICHAEL FARREN

1943 - 2013
Poet, Author, Songwriter, Godfather of Punk

Half Druid, half Tony Soprano,
Half Rochester, half Leonardo,
Half Mekon, half Jabba the Hutter,
Half Paine-in-the-Burroughs, half nutter,
Our cat-loving Deviant Nietzsche,
Has chosen his exit — the preacher
And poet of leather-clad ladies,
Is dining with Elvis in Hades.

THE TREE PLANTER'S REPLY

Your children's children beam at us and smile,
Their impish faces full of love and mirth.
Such photographs! My childlessness a trial —
I claim no progeny by blood or birth
And yet! beyond that wall, for mile on mile,
A million of my children feed the earth.

New York City (55 W. 39th Street) November 5, 2013

It is still a wonder, almost a consolation for me to realise that I have caused to be planted over one million native broadleaf trees in the Heart of England. Hah!

VIKING FUNERAL

This is not the end of the world.
It's just the end of me.
Inevitably,
This burning voyage my last.

Chaos, ruin and rhyme I hurled.
I fought unceasingly.
Vanquished utterly.
My myths shall salt the past.

The anchor catted, sails unfurled,
My barky puts to sea.
Sweet melancholy,
As flames lick up the mast.

New York City (49 St) November 7, 2013

MOVING FORWARD — LOOKING BACK

Moving forward — looking back,
A thing I never did before,
But futures have no path or track,
The past, at least, is trailed by spoor.

Hope is locked in its velvet tray,
Confined where stoics hoard their gold,
(Though I'm no stoic — let's just say
That hope looks best when dying old.)

I do things I have never done,
I speak to pictures, fondle wood
Stroke rugs and handles one by one,
Linger where friends and lovers stood,

Lay down on beds where lovers slept
And wake each morning with the dawn,
Dry-salvaged — all my tears long wept...
A coward, I refuse to mourn.

Candlewood Lake, Danbury   November 10, 2013

REVELATION

There are things men cannot say to one another.
    We are taught as boys: 'Endure; conceal you care.'
This afternoon, my friend spoke as a brother
    And the lover whom I never knew was there.

Candlewood Lake, Danbury November 11, 2013

A close friend of many years came to see me at Candlewood after learning I was terminally ill. Knowing this might be the last time we ever met, he spoke to me as we sat drinking wine in front of the last log fire I would ever enjoy in this cottage by the lake I've occupied for nearly 30 years. He spoke to me as no man ever has before. We parted in tears and laughter, neither of us caring what the waiting limo driver thought. It is a memory I will cling to in the terrible weeks and months to come.

BITTER
On Visiting My Collie Bitch In Her New Home

This is a sad thing — seeing your own bitch
Stretched out and comfortable, in front of a hearth
Not your own. A pup you have known since birth
Now in her new home, scratching an old itch,
Twitching an ear at a half-familiar tread,
Twisting her muzzle, catching sight of me,
And instantly, imprudently, but cautiously
Approaching, brown eyes glistening as her head
Bows and her paw reaches up. Heartbreaking.
How to share the need for this forsaking?
Our lives are not our own on this world's rack.
She is loved here — with a future — a new pack.
'Why did you abandon me this way?'
I wait until she sleeps, then creep away.

Dorsington, Warwickshire   November 12, 2013

No matter how brightly the sun shines or how well things go, the knowledge that you are soon to die twists all inner perceptions to melancholy. But nothing was more surprisingly heart-wrenching than ensuring that my estate collie, Bitter, was adopted by friends in the same village. She went reluctantly, although relatively obediently as always. It is at such times that our inability to communicate with other species causes maximum distress. Bitter has no way of knowing that what I did was for her own happiness. So must the ancient gods have felt, unable to explain to worm-like mortals besieging Troy why their lives must be wrenched and shattered by what appears to be capricious fate. My gratitude to the family who have adopted Bitter (they already have two dogs, a Staff and a terrier) is very real. But seeing her lying in front of a fire in their farmhouse living room, unaware of my arrival, was a dagger in the heart. Why 'Bitter'? Well, there were three collies, once, on my estate, named after beers: Becks, Bass and — Bitter!

THE SUN IS SHINING

The sun is shining,
I'm not in pain,
But, then again — it looks like rain.

And I'm not dead yet,
Plenty to do,
But, then again — who'll see it through,

The verse I'm writing,
The plans I've made?
But, then again — life's light and shade

Will soon be nothing
To me. All gone.
The sun is shining — <u>on</u>, lad, <u>on</u>!

Dorsington, Warwickshire   November 14, 2013

THEY FOUND ME

They found me outside, staring at a field
Of long-horn cows, tears coursing down my face
And asked me why — I smiled, 'My fate is sealed.'
But neither dawns, nor clouds are in that place...

Nor drooping hedges, cows or frost-nipped flowers,
Nor winding lanes, barred gates, nor Quinton Hill,
While soon I shall know naught of mortal powers,
I seek the air while I have lungs to fill,

And fill my senses up while they are there
With London streets, red wine and youth's excess,
Let some seek grace, tranquillity or prayer —
I shun Death's empty peace and seek Life's mess.

Dorsington, Warwickshire November 15, 2013

DEAD MAN LAUGHING

Surreal and scarce believable — a ledge
On which a friend is perched, as on a shrine;
Half gallows humour, half in deadly pledge,
A dead man laughing with us, drinking wine.

Dorsington, Warwickshire   November 18, 2013

Sitting drinking, talking and laughing with a man who is terminally ill and slated to be dead
in months, but who (as yet!) shows almost no outward sign of it, is a surreal experience — as
my friends will testify. There is no 'correct' way of doing it, because we have no model on
which to base our responses. To put it plainly, it's just weird.

A QUESTION FROM ONE WHO LOVED ME
(But Whom I Never Made Love To)

Do I know that I am loved? Not really, no.
Partly because I never could believe
In love. I learned one does not earn it, though,
And once lost is a puzzle to retrieve.
Your question is emotional brinkmanship:
As an actor, world-class liar, stage-struck fraud,
I'd normally deflect it with a quip —
Quick wit was ever readier than my sword.
But as we may not meet again, I'll say
What I have rarely said, though long have thought:
Love's mostly blind-man's buff and shadow-play,
While friendship is an art more finely wrought.
    You'll say, 'Friends love you.' Yes, and so they do,
    But friendship is forged, my dear —
                          blade-straight, steel true.

Dorsington, Warwickshire   November 18, 2013

This was an honest question, asked of me in emotionally charged circumstances. I suppose the answer revolves around one's definition of what love is — a question beyond my powers to answer, But if 'romantic love' was a prime motive within the question, then I feel my response, for once, was completely truthful and accurate, from my own perspective. The post-World War II generation in the West (especially men) found it difficult to express their feelings in emotional matters. My father, after all, had been sent aloft after loading the wings of his aeroplane with death which he then rained down upon men, women and children. Can any generation, having taken part in such terrible events, teach their children that the outward expression of love (especially by a male) is not shameful or weak in some way? On balance, the answer has been in front of us for decades — and the verdict is 'No, they could not'. The last four words of this poem are Sir Arthur Conan Doyle's epitaph.

DAWN 19 NOVEMBER 2013

Dawn. Full moon and a blue slate sky due West.
The East, pink menace creeping through a slot.
Our lives — white frost on fields, young winter's jest
That glitters as it melts, then is forgot.

Dorsington, Warwickshire   November 19 2013

'Life is a jest and all things show it…' goes the old rhyme. But whose jest? And at whose expense?

NOTHING CAN BE THE SAME

Nothing can be the same nor should it be,
The years of semi-slumber have long gone;
My sleepwalk out of reason's milk-wood tree
Has wrecked old certainties of Babylon,
Of Athens, aye, of Newton and of Locke,
Those metaphors of hope in which I joyed,
Of time and relativity's cracked clock —
All such are cannon fodder for the void.
A partial glimpse has scarred my shrinking soul;
Why speak of rest's embrace, of peace or bliss,
What words of comfort can there be to toll
The horrors of unreason's black abyss?
    Our force-fed minds, fat pigs within a sty,
        And we ourselves, mere fragments of a lie.

Mandalay, Mustique May 3, 2014

Grim, but true. For me at least at this time. Of course death will lead to a cessation of joy or pain — or self-awareness of any kind. (One knows this, unless of a religious persuasion.) But my lifetime belief in science, of mankind's 'advancement' over the centuries, is rapidly being replaced by the growing suspicion that all our endeavour has been in vain. These thoughts have burgeoned over the many hours I have spent contemplating what we who believe in science can ever 'know'. Or, indeed, ever 'knew'. And if that is the case, if we are little more than uncomprehending 'fat pigs in a sty', then what was the point of the struggle that began with our ancestors painting bison on the walls of caves, progressed to geometry, writing, and — untold centuries later — to our ability to destroy (albeit temporarily) much of life on earth? I shall keep on gnawing at this in the long hours of darkness, now that sleep evades me on so many nights, and report back later, hopefully in a more positive frame of mind. Teach-yourself-philosophy may seem a bizarre undertaking in my particular circumstances, but it's how I approached an early understanding of poetry and poetics and is at least a course that gives plenty of scope for mental activity to while away long hours.

I AM EKING OUT EACH MINUTE

I am eking out each minute,
I begrudge each passing hour,
I am of the world — half in it
And half beyond its power.

I am shorn of time and hairless,
I am brushed and trim and hollow,
I am jealous of the careless
Who speak lightly of tomorrow.

I am wary of compassion,
I avoid most fools who call me,
I spoon love a meagre ration:
(The tears of friends appal me).

I am snared by each day's beauty,
I am weighing out the present,
I have broken faith with duty,
Though dread is omnipresent.

I grow light — my blindfold lifted,
I know all there is of fairness,
I have learned what I thought gifted
Was the price of self-awareness.

Soho, London   November 23, 2013

TIME DYING

Well — obviously — time does not exist,
And in so far it does, quite differently
For those whose names are rising up Death's list
Than from the wastrel vast majority.
Time is a mortal construct, more or less,
A knotted handkerchief for past events
And those still yet to come. To curse or bless
The length of its duration makes no sense.
Intensity of feeling is instead
The yardstick; thus a prisoner in his cell
Awaiting execution, finds time fled
While pining lovers sup from boredom's well.
    Expanding or contracting, cursed or blessed,
    Time dying is infinity compressed.

Soho, London November 24, 2013

My thanks to the steady-eyed wisdom, expressed firmly but with hints of humour, from my old friend and long-time publisher, Gail Rebuck. In essence, this sonnet is a condensed digest of what she gently shared with me when I informed her of my terminal illness. Her experience with the death of her husband, Philip Gould, a couple of years back has prepared her for such traumatic events far better than anyone else I've met. Philip's book, *When I Die: Lessons From The Death Zone* (Little, Brown 2012) is full of such insights, too.

EIGHT HUNDRED POUND GORILLA

I am the eight hundred pound gorilla here
And I sit wherever I want.

However, it does me little good, I fear.
Other diners edge their chairs away
Although my fur is brushed, my molars gleam,
Claws sheathed and trimmed — they have little to say.
I cannot join in their chatter, nor hold a fork,
And I have a strong suspicion they
Are sniggering at me as they steal a glance,
Understandably nervous, pale faces grey.

I am the eight hundred pound gorilla here
And I sit wherever I want.

Mandalay, Mustique   April 26, 2014

NO LONGER OF THIS TRIBE

No longer of this tribe - how could I be
   Now that the reef between us is so wide?
You in your proud canoes command the sea,
   While I consign myself to wave and tide.

Let none but stalwarts share my waning shame,
   The young so soon forget what elders hid,
I would not have them see what I became —
   Far better that you tell them what I did.

Dorsington, Warwickshire November 28, 2013

I DO NOT LOCK MY DOORS AT NIGHT

I do not lock my doors at night,
Nor do I leave on the light,
Soon, if lacking an alarm
I shall rest secure from harm.

Take the key, remove my chair,
I must now prepare! Prepare!
Practise! Lie down! That's the thing,
Shut all doors, let no bell ring.

Dorsington, Warwickshire   November 28, 2013

THERE ARE ONLY SO MANY GOODBYES

There are only so many goodbyes
    One mouth can make,
        one heart can fake —
With each of them part of me dies.
  Only so many goodbyes.

There are legions of blanks to be filled,
    I strive and scrawl
        to fill them all —
But their meanings are lamed or stilled.
  Too many blanks to be filled.

There are so many hands I would wish
    To hold and press
        to wish 'God Bless' —
But my faith is a log-cracked dish.
  The deed is never the wish.

There are only so many goodbyes
    Two ears can bear,
        a mind can share —
With each of them part of me dies.
  Only so many goodbyes.

Mandalay, Mustique December 2, 2013 9:30 A.M.

STRANDED
(The Fate of The Bearded Dwarf)

I searched my mind today and found
Less ballast than there used to be,
And though the ship itself seemed sound
She lay too still, as if aground
On the shoals of a shallow sea.

Where the mariners, where the crew,
The yards raked slack that once were trim,
As I searched her stem to stern — then knew
There was nowhere left to sail her to,
And if there was, she would never swim.

I mopped and buffed the brass and wood
And coiled the ropes in memory's store
From habit mainly, as best I could,
Then by the logbook, long I stood
And wrote: 'The Dwarf will sail no more...'

But the cabin filled with a ghostly cheer,
And I thought my hardened heart would break
As the hubbub numbed my tingling ear,
And a long-dead mate bawled 'Captain, dear,
There is one last voyage we've yet to make.'

Mandalay, Mustique   March 23, 2014

'The Bearded Dwarf' was the nickname given me by the pioneer staff of my company
in London when we first began our long, piratical cruise in the treacherous waters of
commercial magazine publishing 40 years ago. I used it as the title of a ballad of the same
name in my first book of verse, *A Glass Half Full,* (Hutchinson, 2002). As Dennis Publishing
still has no 'mission statement' (and I hope never will have) that ballad has been substituted
as our corporate raison d'être.

LAST JOURNEY

Our terrors in the saddle,
Our courage in the van,
Our love strapped to the baggage packs,
We ride as best we can.

Our compasses erratic,
Our porters glare and scowl,
Our camels past their breaking point,
The water short and foul.

Our camp tonight in chaos,
Our rations gristled grease,
Our hopes as dull as tarnished brass —
I limp out for some peace,

And open up my notebook,
To scrawl, slumped on a dune,
'The ends of things are broken roads
Yet mostly come too soon.'

Mandalay, Mustique   December 1, 2013

APRÈS MOI...

The sun will rise in the east, a moment's glory.
Small rain will drench new lovers in the park.
A child will beg her father: 'Tell me a story!'
At nightfall, thieves will scout and farm dogs bark,
The wind will rustle leaves on trees I seeded,
The smoke from village fires will scent the air
While neighbours walk their dogs on paths I weeded
Then firmly close the gates I fashioned there.
West Soho bars and nightclubs will be heaving
On narrow streets I trod for forty years.
The world is too much with us to be grieving,
New lovers and fresh beer cures many tears.
This is the way of the world — the way we bear it,
That joy and laughter drowns a soul's dark night,
If I have any luck left, let me share it
With some young scallywag in breathless flight.
Dear Christ — I lived a life of fire and glory
And après moi... the best of luck to all;
The sun will bring the east a moment's glory,
And then sink in the west — and that is all.

Mandalay, Mustique   December 4, 2013

'Après moi le deluge' (attributed to numerous kings, courtesans and politicians around the time of the French revolution — and later).

This was written after I learned of the death of the gifted artist, Martin Sharp, at his home in New South Wales, Australia. Sharp's 1960s and early 1970s posters sold to British students and young people in their hundreds of thousands. It was virtually impossible to visit a university dorm or a bedsit and not find a Martin Sharp poster featuring Dylan, Hendrix or a Legalise Pot Rally on the wall. He also created memorable covers of the underground counter-culture magazine, *OZ*; a satirical magazine he had helped to found with Richard Neville and Richard Walsh in Australia. When *OZ* came to Britain, Martin's influence changed it utterly; all pretence of satire was abandoned and a quintessential rag of 'fun, travel and adventure' was born, often in colourful pages of eclectic art that made it almost impossible to read. For a while, I hung out with him at a flat he shared with Eric Clapton in the Kings Road. Later, Martin began painting edgier work, especially featuring three of his great obsessions: Vincent van Gogh, Flying Saucers and Tiny Tim. Martin taught me to drop acid, to hold a paintbrush correctly, how to listen to music vastly outside my comfort zone (especially from North Africa) and how to play the Jew's harp. He distrusted my business influence upon *OZ* (I had begun selling advertising for the magazine) and joshed me to turn from 'the Darkside' to the wholly creative. What he saw in a young South London lad I never learned — shared confidences were not part of his habitual vocabulary — but all the same he became a mentor to me, of sorts. Difficult, moody, scarily talented, he wore his aristocratic genius as lightly as a feather. Later, Martin was one of the first to read my early attempts at poetry and to firmly, if wryly, insist I continue writing verse at all costs. Martin Sharp was one of a kind.

NOTHING CAN CHANGE

Might human traits mysteriously have changed
Collectively, by creaking slow degrees?
To bait a bear today would seem deranged,
Yet late abortions fill us with unease.
And what is this new web but barb-edged fare
Available to any toddler's tap —
And is it worse to disembowel a bear
Or air beheadings while the 'faithful' clap?
Nothing, nothing can change, except the means;
Nothing, nothing can change, or ever will;
Religion trumps cooperative genes,
The fear of dead gods' hells are with us still.
    Who murders children playing in a school
    But true believers — each of them 'God's tool'?

Mandalay, Mustique December 7, 2013

Do not tell me, a dying man, that religion does not lie at the very heart of most barbarity, cruelty, war and violent death among humanity on this planet. To anyone who has faced death and stared it down, this fact is a blinding glimpse of the obvious. Supernatural belief has killed more people and caused more environmental destruction on earth than any other cause, bar contagious disease. Yes, I am aware of the huge part that organised religion has played in the creation of civilizations and the consolation (false, but truly felt) it brings to many. But when next you enter a church, temple or similar place, perhaps to celebrate a wedding, a christening or its equivalent, or simply to worship a non-existent entity, remember this one fact: that same organised religion and the men (it is always men) who run such institutions, have been responsible for the deaths of hundreds of millions of others over long centuries of pointless feuds. And they are still at the same game today, as a glance at the news will confirm. All their excuses are bogus. All their beliefs are worthless, especially their sly insinuations about an 'afterlife'. All they crave is the power to control the lives of others. And that is the unvarnished, terrible truth of human history.

WHEN RAGE HAS LONG DEPARTED

When Rage has long departed,
       Unfairness on his arm,
Cold Grief has burped and farted,
       and Blames has lost his charm,
It's odd to meet with others
       who'll be here when your gone,
Acquaintances and mothers —
       Christ, how they ramble on,
While pitiless Reflection
       takes Resignation's throat
Absorbing her inspection
       And fetching her her coat,
As weary Care's vagina
       sprouts ears beneath your bed
To catch that last one-liner —
       to publish when you're dead.

Mandalay, Mustique   December 7, 2013

Written in response to a wise fool who asked me to write something funny about dying.
Hah, hah, hah, hah, hah...

QUEER INTERLUDE

Beneath the hammer blow of weeping
    Blotting anvils of despair,
Before the rot and phlegm come creeping,
    Robbing me of sobbing air;
These interludes of poise — these seething
    Doubts that I must play by ear,
Have offered me this chance of breathing
    Life into the lines writ here.

Mandalay, Mustique December 8, 2013

And therein lies a story I have half-alluded to in the first poem 'A Shadow On My Lung' in this verse-diary. It was a Saturday — the 28th of September to be exact. I was walking through the first wood I ever caused to be planted, a small one on the top of a South Warwickshire Hill, named after the chap who planted it for me — Ralph Potter. Feeling a little breathless, for no known reason, I stopped at the edge of Ralph's Wood and rested my hand on a rowan tree. Straightway, without any warning, my mind was filled with the terrifying certainty that I had contracted lung cancer. This would be an extremely rare thing to happen having contracted (and beaten) cancer of the pharynx (the tonsil bed in the throat) less than two years before. Nevertheless, rowans are the last trees capable of speaking to Men, so folklore tells us. I called my doctor and he agreed to see me on the Sunday. It was a brief meeting. He informed me I probably had a slight cold causing my breathlessness and light wheezing. I insisted on an X-Ray. He shook his head and very nearly called me a hypochondriac, but because Dr. Tim Shackley is a good bloke he arranged for me to go to Stratford-upon-Avon X-Ray clinic the next day, betting me £10 they would find nothing whatever. The rest is history. I never collected my tenner, but as I have written elsewhere: 'the heart sees what the mind dares not perceive'. Of course, I know it wasn't the rowan speaking (at least, I think I know!) but perhaps required the excuse of such an odd intervention to force the issue. In the event, I gained months of horrible, excruciating knowledge that I was destined for the knacker's yard. On the other hand, this foreknowledge made the book you are reading possible. Life is swings and roundabouts.

FOOL'S GOLD

The fear I can deal with — just.
Truth is that I must.
But the loss of all control,
Playing a puppet's role,
Sickened me from the start.
Close friends speak from the heart
And beg me to desist:
'What use to clench your fist?
We're all in the same boat here,
Accept your fate, my dear...'
But it won't be they who've died.
I want to feel I tried
  To shoulder heaven's weight
  Before I pass its gate.

Mandalay, Mustique   April 14, 2014

I wanted to see if I could compose a 'sonnet' in strict, alternate 7 - 6 meter (except for the last two lines which must, for historical reasons be of equal beat) while staying absolutely true to my feelings, intent and belief. I especially wished to avoid any apparent straining for effect or rhyme. Whether I succeeded or not is for others to judge, but at the end of an intensive — not to say manic — hour's work as midnight came and went, I felt an exhilaration that is the partial purpose of all creative writing. Then I walked outside under a perfect tropical night sky and toasted the (nearly) full moon with a single malt whisky and slept like a baby!

AS TIME RUNS SHORT

As time runs short, stretched thin, elasticated,
I find that fears enlarge by grim degrees;
This afternoon, heaved out and yet conflated,
My chest ignited dread that will not ease.

How brave we think we are, until pain's trials
Remind us our imaginings are born
Before the test — scant foil for terror's wiles,
When hope can only hold our hand, forlorn.

Belay, then! Might not liquor and soft laughter,
Sweet memories and morphine — and a friend
Not scourge those flights of 'happy ever after'?
With courage counterfeited at the end?

Mandalay, Mustique December 8, 2013

It gave me a turn, I can tell you. The sudden inversion of inflation and conflation within the lungs, like a giant slumping down on you as if on a bean bag. The real concern of course was — and is — is this a taste of things to come?

MANY PARTS ARE FUNCTIONING NORMALLY

Many parts are functioning normally.
Masturbation, for example, presents
No problems — although I have little call
Or energy to work the thing at all.
My stamina, compared to formerly
Is fading. Mental maps still make good sense.

My new cliché, 'the elephant in my breast',
Blots out a vast array of strongish-suits:
My bowels, my speech, my curly hair still thick,
My suppleness of limbs (a life-long trick),
My balance, dreamless sleep, and all the rest
Are as yet unaffected attributes.

Dread I drown in drink — or stolen laughter,
Though there are other times, alone, I own
To sudden, crushing bouts of desperation,
Self-murderous thoughts of joyless liberation
With nothing waiting — nothing ever after.
Alone as I came in. *At peace?* Alone.

But I was born as tough as sun-dried leather.
The genes within my mother's mother's kin
Decided 'fight or flight' long, long ago;
And in my sinking heart I think I know
That I shall fight, though armed with just a feather,
A quill to spill my guts from deep within.

Mandalay, Mustique December 9, 2013

There is a little too much bravado in the last lines of this for me to be truly comfortable with, but I am (literally) writing against the clock, as the strength oozes out of me like maple syrup leaking into a cup tied to an *acer saccharum* tree in early January. Perhaps there will be time for me to amend it later, though I doubt it. It is pretty interesting to note, however, how many parts of my body are functioning splendidly while treachery is afoot in my chest and blood. It reminds me of the time I discovered a wooden building I was constructing on my estate with flames leaping into the sky through a staircase window. The rest of the building was perfectly solid. Doors locked, all the furnishings inside intact, the swimming pool filled with blue water, lights still on in a few rooms, rugs on the polished floor. Within hours, this structure — since rebuilt — was a pile of wreckage, the pool filled with charred oak beams, the mosaic in the pool just visible through the murky filth. That mosaic was the sole survivor of one of the largest fires in Southern Warwickshire in living memory. Retired firemen still speak of it fondly down local pubs as 'a proper bloody fire that Highfield was. Fifteen engines on site.' Perhaps these poems, like the mosaic, will survive my demise. Who knows?

BEAUTY

'Some strangeness in proportion' — Bacon's pen.
'Too rich for use, for earth too dear' — the Bard;
And there is truth in what was written then,
An inch of beauty often bulks a yard.

But seen from eyes that may not later snare
The same conjunction, simpler things can speak,
Encompassing the spheres of foul and fair —
Their very ordinariness, unique.

For what is rare — or soon to be — can bridle
A rose, a face, long shadows — this old mop,
The weight of beauty's majesty lies idle
Until we face the day worn hearts will stop.

All ugliness is beauty, strangely clad,
A truth gods hide, lest Men run raving mad.

Mandalay. Mustique   December 10, 2013

'There is no excellent beauty that hath not some strangeness in the proportion.'
 — Francis Bacon, essay 'On Beauty'

'Beauty too rich for use, for earth too dear.'
 — William Shakespeare 'Romeo and Juliet'

It is true that as time runs out (in truth, it is running out for all living things, but let us leave that thought aside) one's perception of the most ordinary things, especially with sight, sound, smell and touch, is hugely enhanced. My life has been so busy, that the thought of me contemplating an orange pillow resting on a red chair, with the shadow of a venetian blind slanting across both, would have been almost absurd. And I say this as a poet who for years has done everything I could to increase my powers of observation and comprehension. Yet now, I could happily watch the sun shift its shadow across those ordinary objects for a great while. And why? Because it is unlikely I will ever see the same thing again. This is what made those last goodbyes at a railway stations as men went off to war such terrible events. Indeed, some wives refused to see off their husbands and asked them to slip out of the house quietly, not because they did not love them, but because the pain of a last indelible vision would be too much to bear. I had heard this from an old lady in my mother's nursing home, but never properly understood it before. I do now.

LIFE HAS NEVER ASKED
A DAMN THING OF ME

Life has never asked a damn thing of me.
    Have you noticed? It never does!

I was thinking of this as I watched a bee
    Crawl onto a petal — buzz... buzz.

I heard the holy-rollering, the praising,
    The frenzied requests to the Lord

On Sunday as I passed the church. Raising
    My hat, I imagined how bored

    He must be — if he exists —
        with all this fuss,
    When life has never asked a
        damn thing of us.

Mandalay, Mustique   December 13, 2013

OCCASIONALLY, I FORGET

Occasionally, I forget
My number's up — just as I wake
From sleep, then like a fool I let
Old Hope flood in; a big mistake.

Old Hope is an unwelcome toad
Who squats upon your heaving chest
To burble in his book-learned code
Of Resurrection — and the rest.

He means well, long beloved by Men
His claptrap never yet destroyed.
There is a time for Hope — but then...
A time to face the hopeless void.

Mandalay, Mustique   December 13, 2013

Emily Dickinson described hope, somewhat disparagingly, as 'a thing with feathers'. (Forgive me if this quotation is slightly botched; my reference books are not by me.) Others have characterised hope both positively (I have done so myself in my poem, 'The Rill of Hope') and negatively in the extreme. Like beauty, it resides in the heart and mind (not the eye) of the beholder. To raise hopes when there are none is very often the only way friends, relations and certain medical professionals can speak to a terminally ill person — as much for their own comfort as for yours. (Their behaviour reminds me of receiving tear-stained, ten-page, hand-scrawled letters filled with despair and well-meant but misplaced protestations that 'you were the light of my life and will never be forgotten'. What possible good can such an epistle do for the recipient? Such missives are created solely to relieve the anguish of the writer — and more often than one might charitably wish to believe, in the hope of increasing their portion of what you leave them in your will. Harsh? Of course it's bloody harsh, but it's true more often than false.) Or else there is the bunkum of the deeply religious, like the author G. K. Chesterton: 'Hope is the power of being cheerful in circumstances we know to be desperate.' What rot. The power to attempt to be cheerful, by anyone, at any time, is to be applauded, especially in difficult circumstances — it is a form of real courage — but it requires no bogus hocus-pocus especially of supernatural overtones. When the tough are dying, it's time to boot hope out the door and let it find a more comfortable abode, where, indeed, its indefatigable prattling may work wonders on the basis of the placebo effect. But in a hospice or the home of a dying person, false hope has little place. Indeed, it will almost certainly do more harm than good.

APART

Ah! how suddenly one is set apart,
And how pervertedly the fearful heart
Of even the dearest friend or lover
Seeks out camouflage — or runs for cover.
This is not to deny unfeigned distress
Or bravery, or, God forbid, still less
To denigrate that tenderness of feeling
Which bears one up when iron words are reeling
In clouded storms of terror and of dread,
Knowing that one will soon lie cold and dead.
No, this is the separateness unlatched
From life's free paths, when all becomes detached
Of free will's stroll, when curving lanes run straight
As some dark shadow waits beyond the gate,
The servant of a darker thoroughfare,
And there is nothing left to try or dare
But cast a swift look up — then kiss the sky
With one last wink to wish the world goodbye.

Mandalay, Mustique January 18, 2013

This detachment, this knowledge that you are 'apart' from others and grow further apart as
your end approaches, reminds me of my early youth when on entering my grammar school
of 500 boys I found that only one other pupil (in the year above me) had a divorced parent.
Good training for what is happening to me at present. This is nobody's 'fault' (if there is
indeed any fault at all) but mine. But it is how I feel and how, I now learn, many terminally
ill people feel. It's why cats creep out into the bushes to die, and why condemned prisoners
act as they do. Unfriendly, odd and disturbing to all; but, I guess, not so unnatural when you
think about it.

ALL THINGS BREAK

All things break. That is their destiny.
Systems fail. How could they not? The stuff
They are made never quite strong enough.
Whisper it softly, even your love for me
Begins and ends when we have ceased to be.
All oaths to infinity are merest bluff—
Gods come and go; their priesthoods huff and puff
And what is left — the smirk of history.
Are all love's promises, then, faithless toys
If all things break, so necessarily?
Who is to judge? The vow is not the key,
While breath holds death at bay, faith seals our joys.
Do not concern yourself with some forever.
When bridges fall, we sink or swim together.

Mandalay, Mustique   December 19, 2013

Not that it matters a damn, but the form of this 'Italian' sonnet was taken from Sir Thomas Wyatt's 'The Lover abused renounceth Love' written in the early 16th century. Though known almost exclusively for his introduction of the Italian sonnet form into English poetry, Wyatt has always seemed to me to be far more than a mere innovator. At his best, his phrases tumble down the centuries as fresh as an apple plucked from an orchard tree. How rich we are in the canon of poetry written in English (by which I include American, Canadian, Caribbean, Australasian, the sub-continent and the rest) and how lucky the world is to have at its command – formerly in printed anthologies and presently through the internet – this glory of human endeavour (however doomed) dedicated to surmounting the obliteration of entropy.

TGTBT

The thought of rice stirred with a knife
Too sharp to lick or wipe,
Has shaped the grain of half my life —
Too treacherous! Too ripe!

The thought of love stripped of its need,
Defies our wiles to grow,
The seed on which our threshed hearts feed
We reap, but cannot sow.

Mandalay, Mustique   December 21, 2013

To encounter such love is rare; to be a part of it, rarer still. But so as not to tempt the gods,
I did not spell out the title of this short poem, although I am sure you will easily decipher
what the letters stand for.

ON THE THRESHOLD

I wound my thread of luck within life's maze,
  I quaffed my cup, too careless of my fate,
My laughter filled the hollows of my days,
    My dish of faith as shallow as a plate;
      A coward's death I die — in plain despair,
      And I am gone, and yet I shall be there.

I fed those fish that hungered for my flesh
  On scavenged scraps I filched from other men;
I fleeced no virgins, yet my loves were fresh,
  I earned more coin by guile than by my pen;
    A slave to Darwin yields few crumbs to prayer,
    And I am gone, and yet I shall be there.

I searched for meaning, just as most men do,
  My youth curtailed by circumstance and chance;
I learned — and learned most dangerously, too —
    The poor are chained to keep them from the dance;
      My verse I crafted, late as it was rare,
      And I am gone, and yet I shall be there.

Mandalay, Mustique   December 23, 2013

As the distinguished American poetry anthologist, Louis Untermeyer, pointed out in *A Treasury of Great Poems*, first collected in the early 1940s, one of the most moving poems of the 16th century was not to be found in any of the great 20th-century anthologies, including *The Oxford Book of English Verse*. Nor was its author even mentioned in *Encyclopedia Britannica* back then. These omissions have now been corrected, and I am proud to acknowledge my debt for the above lines to the traitor Chidiock Tichborne, who died (by the standards of the time) a horrible but not unexpected traitor's death for plotting the assassination of his queen, Elizabeth I. But the three stanzas of poetry he sent to his wife, Agnes, just before his judicial murder, entitled 'On The Eve of His Execution', will send a shudder of both fear and delight up your spine more than three centuries later. Give it a whirl on the internet — and see if you don't agree.

HOW DIFFERENT IT WOULD BE

How different it would be if I were told
That I still stood a chance of growing old —
Sans that, I have to exercise my heart
Upon an hourly basis, lest I part
From friendly feeling, charity and cheer
For innocents I know will still be here
When I am feeding saplings from below.
You cannot know how hard it is to go.

The mind's dark labyrinth has flimsy doors
For any who might seek to pay off scores;
When there is nothing left to conjure dread,
No fear of a reprisal when we're dead.
What holds us to the core of kith and kin,
While molten chaos churns from fires within,
Sick fantasies that batter at the crust
Of fellowship, of decency, of trust.
None know until they face Oblivion's breath
The danger dead men walking pose — til death.

Mandalay, Mustique   December 26, 2013

'Do not speak soothingly to me of death, glorious Odysseus; I would rather live on earth as
a bondsman to a poor peasant than be king of all the shadows.'
   — Dying Achilles speaking to Odysseus in Homer's *The Odyssey*, Book II

The battles I have fought within my own mind since October 1, 2013 concerning others
around me have made all previous conflicts and terrors childish by comparison.

THE JEST SURVIVES
(For Professor Sea Gull)

The jest survives — the jester is forgotten;
The wit a prince — its midwife misbegotten;

A poet's phrase — the anthem of a nation;
A pauper's grave his fumbled compensation:

> My rope and my scaffold,
> My bed and my board,
> My wife and my floozy,
> My slave and my lord,
> My luck and my Jonah,
> My wound and the salt,
> My slave and its owner,
> My gift and my fault,
> My fable, my story,
> My halo and tale,
> My scandal and glory,
> My home and my gaol...

A line endures — the tribe beyond all weeping;
In darkened caves their bison are still leaping;

The jest survives, with art its pith and kernel;
Each jester lost — no name may burn eternal.

Mandalay, Mustique   December 29, 2013

Much of the inspiration and a few of the antonyms for this poem come from one of my favourite books which I recommend to you without reserve: *Up In The Old Hotel* by Joseph Mitchell — really four books of essays in one, republished by Vintage Books in 1995. Most of the original descriptions of New York City bohemian life in this collection were written in the 1940s and 1950s. A few of the shorter lines in my poem come from a 'real' character described by Mitchell. His name was Joe Gould, a Harvard educated Greenwich Village homeless bum whose life's work was the scribbling of millions of words for *An Oral History of Our Time* in exercise books for decades on end. (There are some who believe that Gould's notes were the sum total of his mammoth endeavour, and that all the rest was a fantasy of his fervid imagination.) At any rate, his epistle was never published, although a few notebooks survive in various NYC libraries and archives. Joseph Mitchell's affectionate nickname for Gould was 'Professor Sea Gull' because of Gould's love of those birds, his habit of flapping his arms and making seagull-like screeches in public or at parties and his (Gould's) claim that he had translated a great deal of poetry and prose into seagull language which his feathered friends well understood.

INFERIOR DISCIPLE

Empty your mind — be less.
Superior
To those inferior
Around you.

Shut out the ugliness —
Babbling throngs
Whose raucous off-key songs
Surround you.

And yet, let me confess,
I'd rather stray
Where peasants piss and pray
About you —

To wallow in the mess
Of life's hard blow.
So sorry — I must go
Without you.

I guess that I was born to wield a pen,
My seed-strewn mind too fertilized for Zen.
This time around,
I'll end my earthly canter
In raucous laughter,
Blood red wine —
and banter.

Mandalay, Mustique   December 30, 2013

NEW YEAR'S EVE 2013

I rearrange books — row on row
As if I shall return,
But there are things too hard to know,
And some too hard to learn.

My fingers team with hand and eye
To set a picture straight,
A choir of inner voices sigh,
'You've left it somewhat late.'

Beyond the gate — a lone bird sings
To drown my daemon's wails:
I always was too fond of things
With feathers, fur or tails.

Mandalay, Mustique   December 31, 2013

How strange to know that this will almost certainly be the last New Year I'll ever see. The fireworks at the Cotton House Hotel, this year, far below my vantage point at Mandalay, were especially fine. But I grow so tired, so quickly now that I was asleep within minutes of the final crescendo.

DID I EVER STOP ONE HEART

Did I ever stop one heart from breaking?
    Emily, truly, I do not know.
Oh, I tried, but life was full of snaking
    Roller-coasters packed with woe;
So many are born with seat belts worn,
    Squirming as the switchbacks twist
Their dangling seats — half bent and torn...
    One I managed, arm and wrist,
To haul back in; she was sobbing, sighing,
    And, Emily, truly, this is so,
She slapped me as she kissed me, crying —
    'Fool! You should have let me go!'

Mandalay, Mustique January 1, 2014

Written in response to Emily Dickinson's poem ' If I Can Stop One Heart From Breaking'

If I can stop one heart from breaking,
    I shall not live in vain;
If I can ease one life the aching,
    Or cool one pain,
Or help one lonely person
    Into happiness again
I shall not live in vain.

Well, I did save one. That is certain. But what is not certain — not at all — is whether I should have made the attempt and whether she truly thanked me in her heart of hearts for rescuing her from a self-induced overdose. I shall never know. She lives, happily enough, so I hear, to this day, but after an initial warming of my bed (perhaps for thanks, perhaps not) she never contacted me again.

IT WILL BE THE LEAVES

It will be the leaves,
And the boles and the bark and the domed sky
Grey against winter boughs, bracket-fungi,
Swollen twigs, puffed catkins, buds as various
As a mad artist's palette — precarious
Nuts and fruit at the utmost top of the tree,
And bracts, and the flowers, of course. But mostly,
It will be the leaves.

And lovers and friends,
Never as many as we'd like to pretend,
But each a beacon of sorts — and in the end
The thing that made life more than marching sore
Across a world where we grew rich (or poor)
And talked and rutted, boasted, stole a kiss,
Fled, led, won or lost. Yes, mostly I'll miss
Lovers and friends.

Mandalay, Mustique January 5, 2014

And perhaps it will be. But the sad truth is I will never know. As no creature knows, will know or has ever known (at least for those of us lacking belief in the supernatural). I have an old friend who argues, kindly, but strongly, 'At least it will be peace.' But this is untrue. Peace is a conditional state requiring comparison with other states to have any meaning. In death, there is no state whatever for what was once a conscious mind. Therefore there can be no comparison — and no peace (or misery, it must be admitted). Poems like the one above, then, are written more to keep one's spirits up than as a true reflection of a considered or recollected inner truth. Even so — it will be the leaves!

WE COME

We come — from either here or there.
We go — but cannot tell to where.

We live — but never learn what for.
We search — but who has found a door?

We preach — but then forget to do.
We blame — half caring what is true.

We look — but mostly dread to leap.
We jest — but jealous djinns lurk deep.

We love — to keep worse fates at bay.
We pray — then jumble what we say.

We dream — suspecting dreams are false.
We dance where angels feign to waltz.

We fear — above all else, we spurn
The void that waits for our return.

                    * * *

Yet birdsong thrills my shivering skin —
And though it should not, hope creeps in.

Mandalay, Mustique January 7, 2014

LOST

This is ridiculous. We were all agreed
We would meet there. I wish to sit with Cook
And speak of circumnavigation; to plead
With Dickens, 'Please, please finish the damn book';
Debate literacy with Sumerian scribes,
Shake the hand of Shelley, take in, more or less,
The marvels of that host of gathered tribes...
And now you tell me you have lost the address.
Stop immediately and ask the way.
There is no one to ask? And as Emily found,
No way of stopping the carriage, no cord
For such emergencies. So where are we bound?
Stuff that! I shall never call any man 'Lord'.
    Kindly search your pockets again. We have need
    Of that address, my friend. We were all agreed.

Mandalay, Mustique January 11, 2014

'Emily' is Emily Dickinson from her poem 'Because I Could Not Stop For Death' and my 'cord' is the old fashioned instrument that ran through passenger compartments on all trains in the 20th century with an imposing sign sternly warning: 'Pull Cord In Emergency Only. Fine for Misuse: £25.' (Which was a fortune when I was a lad.) I longed to pull one, and force the train to brake and stop, but sadly never plucked up the courage or had the money to pay the fine.

I TAKE EACH DAY AS IT COMES

I take each day as it comes. What else to do?
Misery's urn has long-since spilt its tears;
Dull rage still smoulders there; self-pity, too.

I stare at the glass and murmur, 'Is that you?'
Slimmer than I have been for thirty years;
I take each day as it comes. What else to do?

My face not scrawny yet, but showing through
Imposter's eyes are unaccustomed fears,
Dull rage a smouldering glare; self-pity, too.

Each hour an unknown traitor turns the screw;
Ah, Dylan, I would rage, but no one hears.
I take each day as it comes. What else to do?

I keep my secret yoked, save for those few
Whom I can trust — my world filled with fakirs,
My cage a mouldering lair; self-pity's coup.

An albatross of hope that never flew
Bedecks my neck, too close for knife or shears.
I take each day as it comes. What else to do?
Dull rage still smouldering; self-pity, too.

Mandalay, Mustique January 12, 2014

The wonderful thing about a complex form like a villanelle is that it forces the writer to consider, reconsider, weigh and experiment again and again with certain lines until they are as right as the author can contrive to make them. Other lines virtually write themselves. This is when poetry is a joy for a poet — time appears to vanish and the mind is filled with images, words, phrases, myths, half-remembered lines from other poets (dangerous, that!) and a sense of completeness as the long journey nears its end. In my particular, and, let's face it, somewhat peculiar situation, this sense of losing oneself in something one hopes is beautiful, or may have some meaning for others, is priceless. Literally, priceless. There is a reference here to Dylan Thomas with his famous villanelle 'Do Not Go Gentle Into That Good Night', one of the lines of which contains the phrase, 'rage, rage against the dying of the light.' Thomas wrote it (so they say) as his father was dying. Who exactly, was his father supposed to rage at, and to what purpose? Even so, it is a magnificent work. The other passing reference is to the albatross that caused all the trouble in Samuel Taylor Coleridge's 'The Rime Of The Ancient Mariner'. But, of course, you knew that already.

I SEE MORE BEAUTY NOW

One thing; I see more beauty now.
I guess that it was always there,
It's all around us, everywhere.
I'd never noticed it — somehow.

But as the fading has begun
I find it in a stone, a fern,
In log fires where the embers burn —
All beauty fuels its own dark sun.

The songs of birds tear at my heart,
The arcs of waves well in my eye,
My dog's wet nose, a star filled sky...
A consolation? Well, in part.

Mandalay, Mustique January 16, 2014

Nor am I the only one to note this. My friend, Rosemary, who has contracted a form of cancer
I am certain she will conquer, almost took the words out of my mouth as we spoke on the
telephone, she in France, me in Mustique. As a professional writer she found herself amazed at
her increased perception of the beauty of the world following her diagnosis. Perhaps this is a
common phenomenon for those afflicted with potentially life-threatening illnesses?

WAKING IN MY STUDY
I rose from my chair and stepping outside found

Full moon, bride's veil clouds and a blazing sky
Strewn with the most extravagant necklace
Of stars; courting tree frogs seeking a reply;
Confused koi circling in the pond; a reckless
Manicou staring from a rafter beam
Baring cannibal teeth. Halos of light
And shadow, insubstantial as a dream,
Mottling the house and garden grey on white.
In a perfect world we would need no art;
Wind through the reeds our poetry and rhyme;
Lapping waves on a shingle shore our song;
Each mountain range a sculpture we might climb.
All paint, all dance were torn from Gaia's heart,
A forgery of nature all along.

Mandalay, Mustique January 19, 2014

'Manicou' is the local name for a type of nocturnal marsupial, about the size of a large rat, which can climb almost any vertical surface and eat almost anything it can digest. Its prehensile tail, mad pink eyes when reflected by car headlights, patchy (mangy-looking) fur and sharp teeth give some visitors the willies should they ever see one — which is unlikely. In fact they are shy of and harmless to humans and perform a valuable function by eating all manner of discarded food or dead creatures. Their naked larvae-like young must make a perilous climb after birth to reach the safety of the mother's pouch. Later, they can occasionally be seen riding on her back, clinging to tufts of fur. More often, manicou can be heard scurrying about in the void between house roofs and the sarking below. Mustique has a plentiful supply of manicou, but they are rarer elsewhere in the Caribbean because locals consider their meat a delicacy.

THE 'LUNACY' OF VERSE

How far dare poets wander
From truth and commonsense?
A long way, a fair way —
Beyond the gate and fence

Which shield us from 'reality',
From 'otherness' and worse,
A long way, a fair way —
The 'lunacy' of verse

Is what a poet lives for;
Try reading what they penned,
A long way, a fair way —
When trouble calls, my friend.

Mandalay, Mustique January 20, 2014

To those interested in the composition of verse, as opposed to quality (debatable) or purpose (even more debatable) this was written in a huge rush between 9:17 a.m. and 9:37 a.m. (so my computer tells me). I do not even recall drawing breath, painful or otherwise, or anything else that may have occurred around me. For twenty minutes of earthly time, my craft, mind and spirit were in 'the zone'. Prof. Stephen Hawking once said that when he set out on his mental safaris to the abyss of time, one of the last tribes he left behind were madmen and poets. That is their real function. To seek what others do not and bring news of what they have found.

COLD FEET

When I go to sleep now my feet are cold.
This never used to be so.
Perhaps this is a part — or so I'm told —
Of growing old? I wouldn't know,
Having not grown old before.
Or wondered what age held in store.

Tying up my laces is a hard climb.
I'm breathless, pains in the chest.
I've learned a few ways round it for the time,
But it comes with all the rest,
The continuous pretence,
And conversing in the wrong tense.

Perhaps I'm lucky I shall never grow really old.
Perhaps. But when I go to bed, my feet are cold.

Mandalay, Mustique January 20, 2014

I am beginning to become what the quacks call 'constitutionally weak'. Lack of breath plays a big part in this as the tumours in my lungs expand. There is no treatment they tell me, except to attack the tumour with chemotherapy — a risky proposition. I get outside as much as I can, lolling around the veranda with its beautiful views of a turquoise sea and the islands beyond. And I go for trips on my Segway electric scooter, which has performed faithfully on this island, to everyone's amazement, for 13 years. So my balance cannot be entirely shot. But the end of the 'pretence of normality' (as I have called it) is approaching, although I have told very few people on Mustique of my illness. (Too much fuss, however well meant, is exhausting.) Unfortunately, this also means I must begin considering leaving here for the last time, to take the flight to Blighty to finish the job. By the way, I asked the quacks about my cold feet and was told: 'the cold feet are a part of growing older. The breathlessness and chest pain are not.' So there you have it.

This is almost the last poem I'll include in *I Just Stepped Out*. I shall keep on writing for as long as I can, but one must draw a line somewhere if a book is ever to be completed. Today was the 110th day following my terminal diagnosis. I've written more than 90 poems in that time, (a ludicrously high count) from which I will select the best, with help from friends and editors, for the Verse Diary section you're presently reading.

THE LURE

The falcon cannot hear his keeper's cry,
Its loyalty lacks talons and a beak.
The lure alone remains to tempt the eye.

Its hood and tether loosed, it longs to fly,
Not knowing either where — or whom — to seek.
The falcon cannot hear his keeper's cry.

The wind about its wings, why should it try?
Its eye so keen, each feather groomed and sleek,
The lure alone remains to tempt the eye.

The blobs below, so easy to defy;
The weakness of the strong incites the weak.
The falcon cannot hear his keeper's cry.

My soul — this hawk — is tugging for the sky,
Old bonds of love are tumbling from their peak.
The lure alone remains to tempt the eye.

A time to moult, to feed, to breed, to die,
As weariness and hope play hide-and-seek;
The falcon cannot hear his keeper's cry.
The lure alone remains to tempt the eye.

Mandalay, Mustique January 28, 2014

Anyone who loves poetry in English knows where the allusion for this was birthed — in the mind of W.B. Yeats with his 'widening gyre' in one of the greatest of all 20th-century poems, 'The Second Coming'. But I wanted to explore a different theme using the same bird. Did it ever return to the leather strop of its keeper? Can those at death's door choose to return, for a while, to the living? And should they, even if they can?

DOUBTFUL

It's doubtful I could bear another spring,
  The winter in my heart could find no room;
And yet, whatever fate the gods may bring,
  Within my mind, the bluebells are in bloom.

Mandalay, Mustique April 14, 2014

Photograph:
Sebastian Rich 2011

❧ FELIX DENNIS ❦

Felix Dennis was one of Britain's best-loved poets. His poetry has been performed by The Royal Shakespeare Company on both sides of the Atlantic and has enjoyed wide success on radio, in scores of English language newspapers and on countless internet sites.

In 2012 Sky Arts aired an hour-long television documentary focused on his poetry, and organisations as diverse as The Royal Marines, the MCC and The National Trust have adopted his poems for their own use. His hugely popular poetry recitals packed theatres across Britain, Ireland, Continental Europe and the USA.

As a lover of trees, his lifetime ambition was the planting of a large native broadleaf forest in the heart of England. In the autumn of 2013, his charity, The Heart of England Forest, planted its millionth tree.

He had homes in England, the USA and St Vincent and the Grenadines. Felix Dennis died on 22 June 2014 at his home in Warwickshire, England.

For more information on Felix Dennis's life and poetry visit:
www.felixdennis.com

For more information on Felix Dennis's forest project visit:
www.heartofenglandforest.com

Clockwise from top left: Tour Crew, Glee Club, Cardiff, 2008 • Courtyard Theatre, Stratford-upon-Avon, Dec 2011 • Guests at The Northumberland, London, Sept 2010 • Komedia, Brighton, Sept 2010 • The Button Factory, Dublin, Oct 2010.

Felix Dennis performing on his 'Did I Mention the Free Wine? Tours around the world.
Clockwise from top left: Firefly, Mustique, 2001 • Catching forty winks on private jet, US Tour 2004 •
Performing with RSC actors, Gotham Hall, New York, Sept 2004 • Bridgehouse Theatre, Warwick, Oct 2008;
Coral Gables, Miami, Oct 2004 • Wordsworth Trust, Windermere, Oct 2008.

Clockwise from top left: Book Signing at The Hub, Edinburgh, Oct 2010 • The Shaw Theatre, London, Oct 2013 • Tour Crew, Bloomsbury Ballroom, London, Oct 2013 • Bloomsbury Ballroom, London, June 2013 • Sold Out! UK Tour 2010.

Clockwise from top left: The Shaw Theatre, London, Oct 2013 • Bloomsbury Ballroom, London, Oct 2013 • 'Writer-in-Residence', Writer's Cottage, Mustique, Feb 2014 • Felix posing next to his 'Please Go Away' sign, Writer's Cottage, Mustique, Feb 2014 • Felix working on I Just Stepped Out, Writer's Cottage, Mustique, Feb 2014. Photographs: Jenna Adesso, Fergus Byrne and Sebastian Rich (and from Felix Dennis's photo archive).

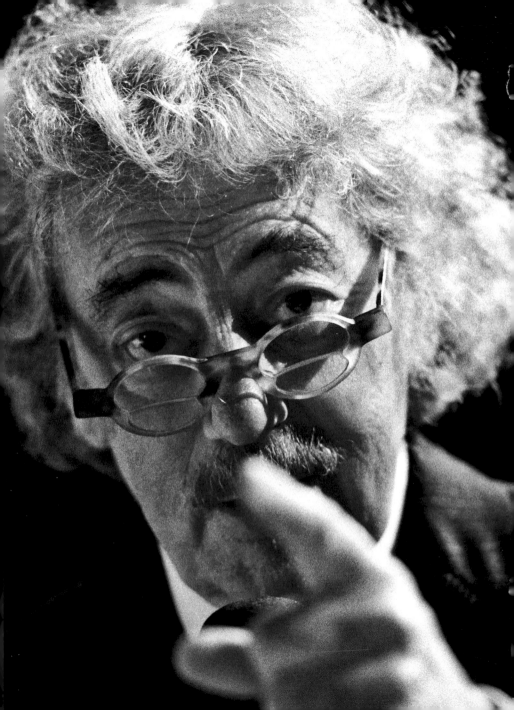

❧ INDEX ❧

ENVOI

'This may be the last time. This may be the last time.
May be the last time, I don't know.'

— The Rolling Stones, 1965

'The Last Time' by Jagger / Richards
adapted from an old gospel song by the Staple Singers.
Recorded in Los Angeles and released by the
Rolling Stones in early 1965
Producer Andrew Loog Oldham
'B' side 'Play With Fire'

THE CARAVAN MOVES ON

Friends die — and we screw our wet eyes up
    And swear we'll miss them now they're gone.
We mourn, then Arsenal wins the Cup;
    Dogs bark, but the caravan moves on.

❧ A NOTE ON THE POEMS ❧

I began writing poetry, unexpectedly, in 1999 while recovering from an illness. I was then in my early fifties — pretty late as these things go. One newspaper journalist has observed that I write 'prolifically and like a man obsessed': perhaps, subconsciously — if indeed there is such a thing — I have been attempting to make up for all that lost time?

I attempt to write for at least a few hours a day on the basis of Mark Twain's dictum that 'most inspiration comes from the application of the seat of the pants to the seat of the chair'. I constantly make notes, having discovered that if a promising line or subject arrives in my head, I must record it immediately — delay is often fatal to its recovery.

For the first few years I found myself writing four or even five poems a week — a virtual cataract. This has now settled down somewhat. I calculate that in the past fourteen years I have spent 15,000 hours attempting to compose verse — nearly 20% of my waking life!

Sometimes I write poetry directly onto my computer. No difference is apparent (to me at least) in the quality of poems created on my computer compared with those begun on paper. When I'm done with a poem, I squirrel it away and try not to refer to it for a year or so. I revise only to make selections for a new book or poetry tour. I always attempt to keep in mind the observation of an earlier poet who wisely pointed out that no poem is ever really 'finished'; merely 'finished *with*' by its author.

Occasionally, I get stuck. Either I cannot write anything worthwhile or I suspect that the form or meter I am wrestling with has usurped the poem's original *raison d'être*. When this happens, I force myself to abandon the blighter and bang it in a folder marked 'Poems In Progress'. In the early days I tended to soldier on, which often led to second-rate work. Other writers have helped me to come to understand that structure is merely a vessel, not the wine, and that spoiled wine in a fancy decanter is vinegar by any other name. I have also learned that a bad poem, or one merely strong in the weak places, is still a bad poem, no matter what the cost of its birth pains.

Some poems arrive effortlessly, others are the result of months of graft. There appears to be (forgive the pun) no rhyme and no reason to it. Sometimes I find writing poetry truly exhausting, mentally, spiritually and physically. On other occasions, especially when I am convinced I have created something worthwhile, I am invigorated even after hours of work.

Audience reaction plays a part in the selection of poems for a new book. While no single audience is infallible, their collective view is nearly so, in my experience. Booze can help in writing, but only for an hour or so after the first glass of wine; later, mortifying gibberish is too often the result. Reading the work of other poets is inspirational, but dangerously beguiling. I love to read poetry, but I now separate that activity from my own verse-making.

What of intent? Do I write poetry to be performed, to be recorded, or to sit quietly on the page? As anyone familiar with the subject will confirm, some of our finest poets are, or were, poor readers of their own work. (To test this, visit the wonderful website created by Richard Carrington and Andrew Motion, **www.poetryarchive.org** which features, alongside much else, historical recordings by outstanding poets.) Even so, poetry is, in essence, an oral art, a form of song older by far than prose. Rhyme and meter developed partly as a mnemonic device — long before hieroglyphs were scratched onto rock or bark.

The answer, then, is that I write poetry to be read aloud while knowing that many of my readers will not do so; knowing, too, that only a small percentage will ever attend one of my public readings. Instead, my publishers include a free audio CD with all my poetry books. Having heard actors from the Royal Shakespeare Company read my poetry on stage, I'm aware that I have neither the talent nor training to match them. Even so, I sit in a studio three or four times a year recording my work. These recordings appear in the audio CDs found in my books, on my own website and others, on the special audio books created by libraries for the blind — and, when I'm lucky, on various radio and television programmes.

Does it all matter? Years ago a lady came up to me after a poetry reading. She was crying softly. As I signed her book, she said: 'How could you know? How could you know? You are not a mother. How could you know?' She squeezed my shoulder as her husband led her into the night. So, yes. It bloody well *does* matter — to me and to her, at least.

While it is idle for authors to feign total indifference to applause or brickbats, all in all, I am convinced I write mainly for myself. One of America's most respected literary critics has called me 'the best poet writing in the English language.' At the same time, a respected London literary magazine has accused me of 'dragging English poetry single-handedly back to the Stone Age'. I try not to spend too much time gorging on 'the glories of triumph or failure' and keep on with the job, whether planting trees in my forest, encouraging young talent to make money (for me and for them) or creating the very best poetry I'm capable of.

I'm pretty sure I would continue to write verse if no one in the world expressed interest. I write to discover who I am, to escape the carapace inherited from a life in commerce, to stave off predilections for other addictions and, primarily, to experience the joy of weaving words to shape ideas and vice versa. As a somewhat noisome beast, perhaps I should have inflicted my verse-making onto the world anonymously, using a *nom de plume* — the very advice I received from well-meaning friends years ago — but to have done so would have deprived me of the pleasure of performing my work in public.

As Lord Chesterton remarked: 'It is hell to write but heaven to have written.' Amen to that, would say most writers. Why then do we continue to plumb the depths of Chesterton's hell? For some, like Dr. Johnson, the answer might be, 'to make a living': (not that I believe him for a minute). For others, 'to make a reputation' or simply, 'because I can'. For me, it is the result of a chance discovery made fourteen years ago in a hospital bed: that the flame of poetry cauterizes the wound of life as nothing else can.

Readers wishing to learn more, or to watch or listen to me performing my poetry, or to read my poems online, (published and unpublished), will find a warm welcome on my website at **www.felixdennis.com**